## 52 Euros

John Gallas was born in 1950 in Wellington, New Zealand. He came to England in 1971 to study Old Icelandic at Oxford, and stayed. He has worked for many years as a teacher with the Leicestershire Behaviour Support Team. He has published eight collections of poetry with Carcanet Press and edited the anthology of world poetry *The Song Atlas* (2002).

# 52 Euros

Containing 26 Men and 26 Women in a
Double A–Z of European Poets,
done into English by
JOHN GALLAS

First published in Great Britain in 2013 by
Carcanet Press Limited
Alliance House
Cross Street
Manchester M2 7AQ

www.carcanet.co.uk

A CIP catalogue record for this book is available from the British Library

ISBN 978 1 84777 099 8

The publisher acknowledges financial assistance from Arts Council England

Typeset by XL Publishing Services, Exmouth
Printed and bound in England by SRP Ltd, Exeter

# Contents

# A Short Word before *52 Euros*

There is only one way for a poet to translate the poems of others, and that is by being himself. The poems in this collection all read, more or less, like me. They could not do otherwise. To work on a poem at the utmost is to call into service all the things that go furthest in one's own abilities. To do less would be unworthy. To mimic fifty-two poets would be only to do the police in different voices. It is better that they appear in the committed translator's Force than that they remain on some incomprehensible and invisible Beat.

The poets and their poems were chosen by whoever wished to choose them. This accounts for the democratic mix of the famous, the less famous, the forgotten and the unknown, the last three categories being the happy means of introducing the new to many via the love of a few. The translators produced word-by-word, line-by-line translations into English. These I re-poemed. It was the method also used for *The Song Atlas: A Book of World Poetry* (Carcanet, 2002).

This collection has therefore no general aim beyond the reading and enjoyment of poems, any such aim that might have emerged being necessarily lost amongst the choices, enthusiasms, versions and advice of over two hundred helpers. They are the chief workers of this book. I hope I have made what they liked and loved, in their original languages, good reading, without any critical judgements or awe.

Here are 248 European poems to read. They have all come through at least three hearts and minds to be made as they are in this book. Now they are ready for more.

John Gallas

# A is for Akhmatova

Anna Akhmatova was born in 1889 in Odessa. 'The poems of a half nun, half whore', according to Minister of Culture, Andrei Zhdanov, her work was (unofficially) banned from 1925 to 1940. Her son, and her first and third husbands, were shot or sent to camps for 'betraying the Revolution'. Akhmatova died of a heart attack in St Petersburg in 1966.

## Muse

I wait, I wait at night for her.
I teeter on a thread.
What is favour, first hope or freedom
to my sweet recorder, my enterer?

She's here. Unshuts her shawl
and looks at me close.
I say, 'Did you tell Dante
all *Hell*?' And she says, 'Yesss.'

## King Greyeyes

Hello again, you limpet, Pain!
Yesterday King Greyeyes died.

Autumn evening, clammy-red,
my husband came home and said softly,

'They brought him back from the hunt. Hm.
Found his body by the old oaktree.

I'm sorry for the Queen. He was young.
Her hair went white last night.'

He fetched his pipe off the fireshelf
and left for his night shift.

Now I'll go and wake up my daughter
and look in her little grey eyes.

And outside the poplars say and swish,
'Your King has left the earth...'


## Evening Time

Music-air in the garden,
unspeakable sadness.
Oysters laid in ice,
sharp, clean sea-scents.

He said, 'I'm *really* your friend!'
and tiptouched my dress.
Those hands touching –
how unlike a hug.

Like a catstroke, bird-smooth,
like a look at a slim lady rider...
a quiet laugh in quiet eyes
under wan gold eyelashes.

And the blue string songs
under gliding brume:
'Thank God in Heaven –
at last you're alone with love.'

## I Warn You Now

I warn you now –
this is my truly last life.
Not swallow, not mapletree,
not reed and not star,

not springwater,
not bell–clang so
will I be back to disquiet people,
or still annoy their dreams
with my whining age.

## The Last–Time Song

My heart went barely cold,
but I walked brightly.
I mistook my left-hand glove
to my right.

I thought, too many steps,
though I knew – only three!
Autumn hissing with mapletrees
tugged, 'Die with me!

I'm skewed with gloom
and wrong black days.'
And I said, 'Sweet one, sweet one,
me too. I'll die with you'…

This is the last-time song.
I saw the dark house.
Just bedroom candles alight
with cool and sallow fire.

## Hands Hitched Under My Shawl...

Hands hitched under my shawl...
'Why so white today?' –
I made him drunk
on woe-sour wine.

How can I forget? He reeled out,
mouth skew with hurt...
Downstairs, hands derailed,
I ran to the gate for him.

I puffed – 'It was all a joke.
Don't leave me, I'll die.'
He smiled, strange and still,
and said, 'Get out of the wind.'

# and for Apukhtin

Aleksey Nikolayevich Apukhtin was born in Bolkhovo in 1840. He wrote poems and tales, and was known as 'the Russian Oscar Wilde'. A critic said that 'his wallpaper was of the Young Officers pattern'. He died in St Petersburg aged 53.

*Ten Country Pictures*

### Dedication

Your grave is still new:
the white, cold storm has never
lapped its raw-wilt flowers with snow:
but I'm sick of life,
joyless, flat,
unwarmed by your breath,
unmixed with your days.
Ah, a child unsees with light –
the far shore shone at me then,
friendly through fog –
I thought… I saw… happiness, a madcap heart,
on my life's busy road…
and – God! – mad, mad! –
shut doors all open –
I swam… but what I saw
on that longed-for shore…
hot, angry, hating…
I cannot write.
And so, with a snapped soul,
dream-fallen,
I stand unsure
by the dark, shut door.
Do I stop on the road?
Do I have it with the hollow men?
Or, swamped in my soul's storm,

go to war unkilled?
Young soldier,
new in the loaded fight –
will I be sure and strong like you
and fall like you in the end?
Wherever your soul is rolling,
happy and unseen of us,
hear these poems, please – my love's work:
I wrote them full of heart.
If not you... Oh God!...
who can I turn to, stranger here?
Still, in your black, busyless grave,
I love you more than anyone.


## Midday

Gold rye slews in the wind
like a wide woolsheet;
dust lifts, thick-walling
the road away.
My heart aches with nameless pain,
past hurt...
Ah, if I could chance on a sudden friend
here, and we cry:
but I cry only with you,
blank fields...
and you are weeping-wet and sour
with it, my own land.


## Country Road

A little track, thin, skew, runs
through Russia, on, on and border-blind,
through forests, rivers, grasslands, cornfields,
on, on, quick-skipping here and there:
there are not many Wonders herealong –
but its lumpy look is sweet and dear to me.
When morning holds the bloomy sky

it dew-shines in a mist;
airbreaths bring the sweet smell
of mown hay from sleepy clearings:
ssh, everything is asleep – in the morning hush
just a gold sea seen shortly in the rye,
and where a freshed eye looks
there is a fluttering stillness, and wide.
Ride to the hill – past it is a village
with a clear green church.
Higher, the Big House...
crack-canted roofs,
no gardens, creeks – in the stunty grove
lime and hazel overgrow apart,
and past it, by the pond, a sluice...
Bare picture! Dear picture!
Reapers tramp sickled to the fields,
birds sing, sing in the limes,
a hackhorse, its shabby hand,
cows cross, hooting.
It's hot... day lifts, redder, redder, a little, a little.
Ride to the bigger road –
there a cartcreaking loadline, crackwillows,
and along the blazed way rattling
this news and that news from other lands...
and there, little Russian track, you whisper away.
A little track, thin, skew, runs
through Russia, on, on, border-blind –
at the wide road, a gate ahead,
behind, dust and milestones... look, on the right,
there, my path rolls again like a patterned ribbon,
fitful, wayward.


**Songs**

May outside... sowing started,
ploughman walks behind his plough...
I hear my home's dear tunes
with black sadness.

Not a dull, soft mourning –
end of an endless ache –
I hear a something-else in my home's dear tunes.

Bravely well the sad songs,
filled with a youngman's strength:
years of pain, and pain
piled in them, huge.

And it seems, at the first yell,
they break their irons and hurl
to the holdless plains, the endless cornfields,
the inmost of giant forests.

Ah Russia! Downcast in want!
Unhappy land…
I do not believe that freedom's song
is kept from those fields!


## Summer Rose

So late, so mean – why have you
not flowered, oh Eastern girl,
sweet stranger, here?
The gold May nights
have shimmer-sped,
the gold spring days.

Look, here in sun-shadow
the nightingale stayed for someone,
singing, singing his loving-song:
singing so quiet, so sweet,
so deep without hope,
about betrayal!

You should have flowered then:
as if, by a miracle,
the song had bodied,
bloomed with sadness –
then how the wing-singer,
blushed in delight,
would have longed at you!


## Yesterday at Windows...

Yesterday at windows we sat in silence...
the glittering stars, the nightingale's ebb-song,
leaves whispering in,
this ease and fear... all this, all this
has long been the song of others, I know,
and long been our usual mind.

But I shook in a dreadful dream:
I was looking for something, something past,
eager and feared, begging for sleep and forget...
but the answer – bright, glared stars
and the far, loud pule
of the singer of passing Spring.


## Girl Sadness

Got hot, can't sleep...
the moon, redface-
full, lours in
the low window.
The fields are hush,
everyone in bed;
on the small wind
I smell hemp,
mist-in-a-sheet
on the darkened road...
tears or nightingales –
can't sleep.

Got hot, can't sleep...
sleep strained out of my eyes,
something starts
in the heart that is me,
like someone is crying,
moans, back somewhere...

Head-worries,
chest-stone,
overhot, want to
hug – who?
Don't know.
Can't understand.

Tomorrow is Sunday,
guests coming,
take me to the village,
the church –
in thick tanglewoods
a wedding will... will –
how many tears shed sour
in the night.
Sadness, sadness
stuck till day ...
if they knew
what I ...

That yesterday I got up,
went to the ploughed field,
saw a boy
from the next village –
want to know, to know –
ah, he didn't dare,
not a word, not a word,
just looked...
and now
my soul cranes, and pain...
while my grey and promised man,
smiling, shakes hands...

When the first sun
lines through the mist
I will get up
and past the gate...
no, no, can't tell,
how can I tell... father...
brother will shout and swear,
mother half-kill me...
Got hot, can't sleep...
the moon, redface-
full, lours in
the low window.


## Neighbour

Yes, I love you, my ample neighbour,
when, oozing iron goodwill,
and suavey step, you come to lunch
with an umble-putty smile.

I like you – sugar-voice,
your full, fat flourish and godly thoughts,
and the gentle, burbled, easeful flood
of your tootling talk:
sometimes your thoughts are calmly High,
sometimes fidgety, e.g.
when considering – milkily-acidly –
the misways of the old beadle,
and the younger generation...

And, listening long, I doze away
in your say-say sounds... and in a daydream
I seem to have sat in the big dray-cart:
under the stout horses' steam
I dangle along Main Road.
I come to an empty lane –
no posts, no signs, no hills, no traffic –

no crackwillows,
no cart–caravan,
all smooth and dead: thick dust everywhere…
but the grey tracer and his fat buddy
run short-stepped and screwy down the boiling road
and I, half-dreaming still, rock peacefully.


## Little Place

Ah, little place:
I knew you long ago.
The same far, faint songs,
the same songs meadow–echoed.

And the earth wide around,
all forest shades:
and soon, sickle-shaved,
the rippled fields will lie
in grainy stacks.

But like the riping field
your reapers do not flower:
their fathers' long-borne lot –
terrible, animal,
grinding, slaves.

Your land does not shine
with the soul's fruit:
but hot with tears,
bloodstreamed,
your fields are fed.

Ah, brothers, don't despair –
get ready – nearly now –
the black time will end,
the irons, rotted through you,
will fall from your backs.

There will be a midday hush,
there will be a sun-time…
and on that sweet day
gather your fieldcorn happy and whole
and sing till morning!

Ah, then, then your turn will come,
all fellow-felt! Ah, then,
over the little place
goodness' gathered gleam
will shine from the free-faced sky!


## Goodbye to the Village

Goodbye, my own quiet place, where I,
unbothered and daydream-still, spent days of green study.
Thank you for your quietness, your smiling hush,
your soul-stir.

Ah, I look at the treefields, the far forest
for the last time, flurried and sad:
a different beckoning rushes me off,
other skies are waiting.
And if, one day, I come back to you,
beaten by life, fooled by dreams, the Prodigal Son,
what old friends will I find,
and what new?

And you… my own land: what will I find?
Will your people remember hard old days?
Will I, seeing my own sun set,
watch your gladful morning?

# B is for Boye

Karin Boye was born in Gothenburg in 1900. A troubled soul – about religion, lesbianism, and her sanity – she underwent psychoanalysis in Germany and Sweden. Though her work was considered 'alive, natural and sure', she killed herself with an overdose of pills after walking out into a country night.

## The Fern Owl

Hushed, half-waked summer night
mulls in unheard dreams.
The tarns' shone water
shows the sundown sky's
wan, long space.
The stars whiten away.
Far, far off
the fern owl
jars alone its toneless, spriteless song of sleep.

Unbrave, she does not soar, not up,
but hangs lowly and low.
Featherdown duskwings
as if tied to the earth,
weighted with dust and soil.
Ah, whose two wings
cannot lift him
just drifts, drifts,
pulled beaten to mud, in its colours.

But the whitest white shining swans
that fly their royal roads
in morning's bright air
have not, have never that longing
the fern owl has.
Ah, nothing knows such longing

for far away
as the fern owl
for the all-asking, all-shifting sky.


## Tree

When my door is shut and my lamp is out
and I sit lapped in evening's breath,
I feel around me, around me brush
branches, tree branches.

In my room, where I am only,
the tree spreads lint-soft shadow.
Lives quiet, grows well,
becoming what some Un-me plans.

Some force-Thing, some hidden Push
has laid its will in the treeroot store.
Sometimes scared, I uneasy ask:
And are we friends, and safe?

But it lives calm, grows on,
not my work, not my where.
Sweet and spellbound, to live so near
someonething unknown…


## We Sleepy Children

One white sail slides at the louring shore,
like a tired trailing bird for its night nest,
and up there in the widening sky a glowed evening cloud
drifts blank, like the start of sleep…

And now we turn again, we sleepy children, back home and near,
and smooth thought from our faces, doing from our hands,
and leave them to wan like forgotten games, loose them for real things,
and bend blind-faithed to a strange mother's knee.

## My Skin is Full of Butterflies

My skin is full of butterflies, shudder-wings –
they flutter at fields and have their honey
and shudder home and die in sad little twitches,
and no pollen shifts at their light feet.
For them there is sun, hot, huge, older than old…

But under skin and blood, marrow-deep,
beat the heavy heavy pounded sea-eagles,
widewinged, that never loose their prey.

How for your jangle in the sea-summer storm?
How for your yell when the sun smelts yolky eyes?
The cave is shut! The cave is shut!
And between talons wring, white as cellar-sprouts,
my inmost powers to stay.


## After-Dead

'How does it feel when you get your wings mum when you're
dead?'
'First your back warps – and goes wider and bigger.

Then it gets heavier and heavier. Like carrying a mountain.
Your ribs and spine and marrow judder and burst.

Then it goes straight, wham! and carries the lot. The lot.
And then you know that you're dead and live new-set.'

## and for Baudelaire

Charles Pierre Baudelaire was born in Paris in 1821. A writer, according to a not unusual critic, of 'ghastly, putrid rubbish', Baudelaire drank heavily, took opium and laudanum, and died in 1867.


### Cat

My dear cat, come to my hungry heart;
sheathe your pawclaws
and let me plunge into your gorgeous
metal-and-marble-mix eyes.

When my fingers fondle your head
and your sprung back, wander-slow,
and my hand, lushed in pleasure,
gropes your electric body,

I see my woman. Her look,
like yours, amiable animal,
deep and cold, split-slices like a spear,

and, all along, all around,
her dark body swims
air-faint, and a dangerous sweetness.


### Cats

Mad lovers and strait eggheads
both – in their middler age –
like cats, strong and gentle, house darlings,
cold-cautious and unmoved, like them.

Friends of knowing, and hot love,
they hunt the silent fright of darkness;
Erebus' picked black runners –
if they would bend their pride to go unfree.

Daydreaming, they take the high figure
of great sphinxes stretched deep-alone,
that seem to lull in a lineless sleep;

their spawning loins ball with magic sparkle,
and gold speckles, like small sand,
dim-glitter in their covert eyes.


## Owls

Under the black house-yews
the owls file themselves
like strange gods,
darting their red eyes. They ponder.

Flickerless they stay there
until the glum hour when,
shrugging off the slanting sun,
darkness takes the place.

Their stand suggests, to a thoughtful man,
that we should turn away from
the tumult and twitch of the world.

A man high on a passing shadow
will always carry the charge
that he wanted to change his spot.


## The Albatross

Gobs shoot at albatrosses for fun.
Whacking seabirds. Lull-lifting
trip-trackers that shadow
the shoofing ship through soulcold sloughs.

Dumped on the deck
these sky-kings are gangled and shamed,
and dangle and drag their great
white wings like oars,

this soared traveller, so flying-fine,
halt, slack, their ugly joke.
One bibbles the beak with his corncob,
one hobbledy-mocks the flop that flew.

The poet is like this lord of the clouds,
storm-used, all baggers beneath.
Exiled on the hooting ground,
he trammels in his thundered wings.


**Undone**

The Devil is always nudging near me;
he dips round me like an aery hint;
I breathe him and he burns my lungs
and fills me with bad old longings.

Sometimes, knowing my Grand Art-Love,
he comes as a slinkiest woman,
and, with some winking blue excuse,
enhabits my lips to shady doses.

Thus he takes me, clean from God's sight,
panting and broken-worn, to the middle
of wide, bare, Boredom Plains,

and throws in my tangleful eyes
sleazy clothes, blooming wounds,
and the bloody works of undoing.

## C is for Corinna of Tangara

Corinna was born around 200 BC. She wrote poems, lyrics and epigrams for performance by choirs and girls. Known as 'the Fly', but also as 'the loveliest woman around', she is said to have defeated Pindar five times in poetry competitions. A statue was erected in her memory in her home town.

### 9 Remains

I
killer killer…
kill kill his heart told him…
ah but he hid away…
and presented his presents…
they fire-bombed…
aboard fast-forwarding…

II
Fabulous huge Orion
sure drumbled him, and then named
everything everywhere after Himself

III
lovely Dawn departs Sea's
sea, and pulls the sacred
shine-o'-the-moon out of heaven,
meanwhile sugary Zeus sparkles the Seasons
amidst all the springling flowers
and the waits waddle weary
up 7 Gate City

IV
Envy. Hm. He won't
hurt you on purpose.

V
Well if you ask me I think
Myrtis was an idiot to take on
Pindar I mean she's a *woman*

VI
we you sleep too much. God, Corinna,
you never used to be such a

VII
Notwithstanding, I… splendours of
splendid men and women

VIII
I am called, called by Terpsichore
to warble lovely poems
to the white-wearing Tangara girls,
and they (my velvety-chattery songs, not the girls)
bubble the city with happiness.
Whatever the act…
sits…
the big dancing earth.
And I garland with words
our faded fathers' stories
for our girls. Start here.

Often I have titivated
Cephisus (old old ancestor)
with Vocabulary,
and, oftener, orgulous Orion
and the fifty orgulous
sons he begot upon
slumber nymphs
and luxurious Libya…
the girl… gorgeous… the world she…
bore… begot…


IX
Ah, oh, Thespia: gorgeous children, lovely to strangers,
Muse-beloved!

## and for Carducci

Giosuè Carducci was born in 1835, in Pietrasanta. Anti-God and anti-clerical, he was known as 'Pig Poet' for his rude reviews of others' work. He won the 1906 Nobel Prize for Literature, and died in Bologna in 1907.

### Autumn Morning at the Station

Lights shadow each other,
brightless behind the trees,
yawning their haze over mud
through raindropped branches.

The train is coming. It whistles –
whine, hard, tinny. The
bleared sky, the autumn morning
holds us like a great ghost.

Where? Why? – these people hurrying
at murky carriages, wrapped up
and wordless: to what unknown sadnesses,
what hurt hopes.

Lydia's thinking too, giving her
ticket to the spindle-fingered guard,
and her beautiful eyes, split seconds
of sweetness and memories, to Time's tick.

Railmen come and go at the long,
black train, black hoods,
like spooks; with a pale lantern
and iron hammers, proving

the iron brakes, that toll back
a long, gloomy clang: a worn echo
answering sad from its soul's deeps,
like a jolt of pain.

And the doors' slam shut is an insult;
the last call, just a
quick noise, is a sneer:
rain batters, batters the windows.

Now the monster snorts, knowing
its metal soul, judders, blasts, wides
its fired eyes; huge through the murk
it gushes its whistle to dare space.

The grim monster pulls out; takes my love
with its vile carriages, wing-thumping.
Ah, the white face and the smart veil
go, waving, into the dark.

O sweet rose-pale face,
O brimming, hushed eyes, O white,
clear brow, sweet-set,
leant amongst thick curls.

Life shook in the warm air,
summer shook – when they smiled on me:
and the new June sun
liked to kiss lightly the soft

cheek among a chestnut gloss
of hair; and my dreams,
fairer than the sun, folded
her sweet self too, like a halo.

Now I head back in the rain,
through the fog, and wish they'd cover me;
I trip like a drunk and tap myself
to make sure I'm not a ghost too.

So many leaves, falling, icy,
endless, silent, heavy, on my soul.
I think only, forever, for everything
in the world, it is November.

Better for the man who has lost his senses,
better this shadow, this fog:
I want, I want to drift,
mindless, endless.


## Mountain Morning

In the huge alp-circle, on the bleak,
bleached granite, on dazzle-glaciers,
midday reigns, serene, intense, immense,
in its great silence.

Pines and firs, wind-breathless,
stand straight in the sun that stripes them,
and only the faint, rock-running water
sounds, with a small zither-trill.

# D is for Droste-Húlshoff

Annette von Droste-Húlshoff was born in Westphalia in 1797. First published at the age of forty, she was a poet of 'gloomy mysteries, heroics and death'. The most anthologised German woman poet, she died in Meersburg in 1848.

### Dead Lark

I was at your borderland,
your green-sprigged woods,
and on the first bright streak of sun
your song streamed down;
humming up to the sun
like a midge at light,
song like a squall of blossom,
wingflap like a poem.

I thought that I must trouble too
up to the tender day,
as if I had heard my own singing,
and my own wing sound;
the sun sprayed spark and gleam,
my face blazed and burned,
I reeled myself drunken
like a midge at light!

Then sudden it fell, fell and down,
like a dead coal to the crop.
I saw the wee limbs twitch
and went closer, afraid.
Your last song dying
you lay, a poor cold scrap,
all-fluttered, all-sung with light
by your half done nest.

I could cry for you,
pushing this pain in my heart,
for my life will fade from me too,
I feel it, all-sung and all-burned.
And then my body, poor scrap –
just a greenwood grave
and near, now near my nest,
in my quiet home.


## The Boy on the Moor

O it's spooky crossing the moor
when it's swirly with fen and fog,
and mists curling like ghosts,
and netty fingers in bushes,
and a squirt shoots up with every step,
and the soft chinks hiss and sing,
O it's spooky crossing the moor,
when the reed-ranks cackle in the wind.

The shivering boy clutches his schoolbook
and runs like a hunted thing;
over the flats the hollow wind hurries.
What hacks in the hedges?
It's the Otherworld Diggerman,
who drinks off his master's best peat;
Oo Oo a mad-cow moan!
The wee boy cowers in fear.

Stumpstands stare off the bank,
the pine tree nods like a weird,
the boy runs, ears all aware,
through giant stalks like spears;
and things dribble and swish in there!
It's the Unhappy Spinner,
it's Cursed Leonore
winding her wheel in the reeds!

Go on, go on, running and running,
little–devil–chased;
it burbles in front of his feet,
and squeals under his shoes
like a spook-tune;
it's the traitor Fiddleman,
it's the thief-fiddling Knauf
who nicked the wedding groat.

The moor bursts, and a moan
comes out of a gash hole;
Argh argh Damned Margaret yells;
'O O my poor soul!'
The boy jumps like a struck deer.
If his Guardian Angel hadn't been near
his bleaching wee bones would be left
for a digger to find in the smouldered moor.

And slowly the ground gets harder
and there, by the willow tree,
the lamp twinkles homely.
The boy stands at the edge.
He breathes deep, and takes one
last shaky look at the moor;
Uh-huh it was scary in the reeds,
O the fen was full of frights!


**From the Heart**

All my talk, and each word,
and every touch of my hand,
and my eyes' loving looks,
and all that I've written:
it is no breath, it is no air,
and not just jerking fingers;
it is my heart's burning blood
bursting out through a thousand gates.

## To My Mother

I'd really like to have written a pretty poem
about your love, your faithful ways;
I'd like to have spoken of your gift
of always looking after others, so it is known.

But when I thought of it more and more,
and made all the rhymes the way I wanted,
the heart's flood rolled over them,
scattering my soft song's waves.

So take this plain and simple present,
brought with plain, untrimmed words,
and my whole soul with it:
when you most feel, you know to say least.

# and for Dehmel

Richard Fedor Leopold Dehmel was born in Brandenburg in 1843. He was partial to Nietzsche and climbing mountains, and his poems became favourites with composers such as Strauss, Webern, Zemlinsky, Schoenberg and Weill. Rilke said, 'poems broke out of him as out of a mountain'. He died in 1920 from a lingering World War wound.

## On the Seashore

The world turns still, your blood bells;
the far-off day drops
into its gleamed deep,

shudderless, its glow wraps
the topmost land; far-off night
grapples in the sea,

dragless, a small star rises
out of the ocean, your soul drinks
endless light.

## Parable

There is a well called sadness,
pure happiness flows out of it.
But if you look in the well –
horror.

You shall see, in the deep water pit,
your light-picture, framed in Night.
Drink, and your picture shivers away:
light wells up.

## Night Gleam

The white moon softly
kisses tree branches.
A whisper haunts
the leaves, as if the wood
leaned and hushed to sleep:
my love –

The pond is calm,
the willow shimmers.
Its shadow flickers at
the water, and the wind
frets in the trees:
we dream – dream –

The distance shines,
calm.
The pale levels lift
their damp brume
to Heaven-edges:
there, there – O dream –


## Night Awe

Careful, the light-tide flows
from the moon's wan hand,
clouds to earth,
damping all my fire.

A stray gleam drifts
through woods to the river,
and the dark water shakes
under its kiss.

Can you hear me, heart? The ripple
breathes, kiss kiss me.
And doubtful-strong,
girl, I kiss you.

## Looking Up

A down-weeping willow
hangs over our love.
Night and shadows round us both.
Our faces bowed.

Wordless, we sit in the dark.
A creek used to splash along here.
We used to see the stars sparkle.
Is it all dead and dull now?
Listen – a mouth, far-off – the cathedral –
bell-waits... night... love...


## Thought Landscape

Your face flooded in shine,
a vast evening clearness,
you always looked away from me,
at light –
and my shouting cry's echo died far down, far down.

## E is for Espanca

Florbela Espanca was born in 1894, in Vila Viçosa. She studied
literature and law at the University of Lisbon, married three times, and,
emotionally unsteady, having suffered doubtful health, two miscarriages
and deaths in her family, died on her thirty-sixth birthday, after two
suicide attempts.


### To Be a Poet

To be a poet is to be higher, to be greater,
than Mankind! To bite like a kiss!
To give freely though you are a beggar,
as if you were the King of Above and Past All Hurt!

To have the glory of a thousand dreams,
and not know what you dream of!
To have within a star that burns,
to have the condor's wing and claw!

To hunger and thirst for Forever and Far!
To wear a helm of gold and satin mornings...
To contract the world into one cry!

And it is to love you, feveredly...
It is your being soul and blood and life in me,
to tell it in a song to all the world!


### Our Love

Book of my love, of your love.
Book of our love, of our breast...
Slowly, carefully, open its pages,
as if they were the petals of a flower.

Know that I cannot write another
more sainted-sad, more perfect.
Do not pick the lilies it is made of,
for I have no more in my garden of pain!

Our book, and ours alone! Just mine! Just yours!
Smiling I say, smiling you say:
Our lines alone, how fair they are!

Ah, my love! How many, many people
will say, as they gently close the book:
'Our lines alone, lines of we two!...'


## Day Dawns

Night pales. Day breaks...
The fountain's laughter is louder...
Over the hushed city, the horizon
is a strange, flowering orchid.

Now there are swallows to say
the Mass at Dawn, on the sun's first light.
Rooster-crows call from hill to hill,
fervid with life's joy.

Far off, steps... a dim figure vanishes...
In every shadow Columbine plays false...
Silence circles, eager to speak...

And the fainting, tortured moonlight
remembers pale, giddy, ragged,
a Pierrot, weeping, all in white...


## My Death

When I die, please bury me
beside the sweet and gentle Sea,
whose pained devotions' midnight voice
will be the last prayers for my peace...

My Ocean friend that helps me sleep
will rock me in my final cot.
I tended, all my life, my Life,
and never smiled upon a dream!

And you will come... I know you will...
And I will wake from quiet sleep
and look upon your eyes once more!

The moon will softly say to me:
Be not afraid... Oh sleep... it was the Sea
that sighed... be still... for it was nothing...

The shady, shapeless moon
is a gigantic diamond
set in sapphire blue...
the shady moon
floods along the street...

Ah lying Souls,
cancerous Souls
of virgins who have never leaned
from windows to see roses,
carnations, lilacs, verbenas...

Ah gangrenous Souls,
slave Souls, base, mysterious,
cruel, hallucinating, shadowed,
all in dark and shortcut skews,
made of leavings,
sharp as thrilling
cries like shrieking!
Souls where boundlessness is lost!...

Tragic souls of ugly women
who never have believed
in kisses and a man to wed...
and said goodbye to
worlds of chimeras
and hands filled with dreams!...

Oh Souls of murderers who died
and laughed and killed!
Souls of claws enslaved
in virgin flesh for lust!
Souls of pride and lucency
cut in diamonds!
Souls of tiger-cats, and Souls of beasts!

Oh you who are dazed with chimeras,
Oh depthless wells!
That bear in your tormented eyes
the sap of Spring…
and all the terror of the World!…

Oh bohemian Souls that shine,
that do not know there is a Sun,
hissing Souls
that rake the sea like lighthouse light!

Oh Souls of poets, grim,
sacred Souls
of all there is to sense!
Astonished Souls
that blaze impassioned,
but do not burn themselves!

Old ladies' Souls that wish to please…
Souls of ever-cheating lovers…
Oh Souls of thieves
that galaxies pass by amused!

Souls of vagabonds
at pools and lakes,
swamps and mud…
where fire ascends,
where whole worlds quake
and all things die…
and dreams… and the touch of love…

Souls without Land,
Souls without Kings,
without Faith or Law!
Fallen angels' Souls,
Souls that crouch apart, to groan
like wounded lions!

Come, all of you, to my voice,
for the world is desolate,
and we are all alone.

You who are like me,
Oh Souls of lies!
Come to my window, to my street,
to see the shady moon,
the shapeless moon,
the bright, gigantic diamond
set in sapphire blue…

And surely this parade will pass by here…
along my street runs laughter,
the heady laughter of dawn!
And everything is white!
The untucked wing of a dove!

The lilacs and roses are all white…
The gold mimosas shine as silver now,
and there are lilies beyond count,
sheaves, armfuls…
all is white, Oh God!

And here the lace-decked Angels come
with innocent and gleaming eyes…
and in the air I taste
a vast field of strawberries,
unkept and wild…

And now the virgins! See, what smiles!
They are come new
from Paradise…
and all the air
seems washed afresh
at break of day…

And feathers fall in flurries from the sky
as light as birds…
all sweet and soft…
the white lilies bow…

In silver hands the Gospels come,
the houses shrink before the moonlight…
are they… who can tell… do they kneel?…

The air is pure…
a crystal temple
where, aspin,
there silent passes,
like the wings of doves across the threshing floors,
the gasping Royal Standard,
and the pennants, and the flags!…

Who comes? Who comes?
The parade has vanished with a breath…
Silence! Nothing! No one!
The wonder of dead things!
Hallucination!
And my heart
begins to beat upon the gates…
And no one opens them!
No one! No one! No one!

# and for Eluard

Paul Eluard was born in Saint-Denis in 1895. He suffered all his life from TB, and met his first wife, Gala, in a Swiss sanatorium. He was a member of the French Communist Resistance, and admired Stalin. He died in 1952.

## Little Right-Things

I
Up on Chortle House
a bird laughs up its wings.
The world's so light
it's come unstuck
and so happy
it's all right there.

II
Why am I so lovely?
Because Master washes me.

III
Your eyes change me like moons do
and sometimes I'm lead and sometimes I'm feathers,
a weird black water that fits you,
or soft victory in your hair.

IV
One colour Mrs, one colour Mr,
one at the breast, one at the hair,
the passion-mouth
and if you see red
the loveliest is at your knees.

V
Was she made of stone,
to make Mrs Sure laugh?
She'll dissolve.

VI
Even the Runaway Monster smells the feathers
of this birdie singed with gunfire.
Its ooooow shivers the length of a tear-wall
and eye-scissors slice the tune
that sprouts now in the hunter's heart.

VII
Nature is trapped in your life-nets.
The tree, your shadow, shows its nude flesh: the sky.
It has a sand voice and moves in wind,
and everything you say slips behind you.

VIII
She always says No to knowing and hearing,
she laughs to hide her fear from herself.
She's always walked under the nightarches
and everywhere she's been
she's left
the dint of broken things.

IX
What a face will come on this broken sky,
on these softwater window panes – a booming shell,
to say that the love-night is butting the day,
open-mouth glued to shut-mouth.

X
Not known, it was my favourite shape,
that lifted me from manly worry,
and I see it and lose it and put up with
my hurt, like a little bit of sunshine in cold water.

## XI

Men that change and look alike
have, in the course of their days, always shut their eyes
to scatter the fog of scorn
etc.

# F is for France

Marie de France was probably born around 1150. Writing in Anglo-Norman, she produced lays, saints' lives and a version of Aesop's Fables. Denis Pyramus, a critical monk, pronounced that though her lays were 'not at all true', they were read and loved by many.


## Goatleaf

Hello, here we go, the Tale of Goatleaf
just how it happened, my pleasure,
honestly, truly, cross my heart,
all the whys, wherefores, whats and howses
got from Several Serious Spoken Sources
and a book.
'Tis all about Tristram and the Queen
and their lovely pure Love
that made them miserable and miserabler
and then they died on the same day exactly.
King Mark gets mad about it, their Love,
he is sad and angry at Tristram Nephew
and banishes him to Beyond
because he loves the Queen
and he Tristram goes to South Wales
where he was born
and lives there for a Whole Year
without seeing her oh dear,
so then he is ready to Risk It All,
Death and Destruction,
but not a surprise surely because
a True Loyal Lover
has a terrible time, gets depressed
when he can't get what he wants, that is the Queen.
Tristram suffers and thinks about her
and leaves his homeland
and heads straight for Cornwall

where the Queen is supposed to be,
and he creeps around all alone in the forest
and keeps out of everyone's way,
then he creeps out in the evening light
when everyone goes in for the night
and he finds somewhere to stay
with peasants and poor people
and asks them what news,
such as what is the King doing.
They tell him what they have heard,
the Barons are summoned to
come to Tintagel
where the King wants to have a Court,
Whitsunday Pentecost, well
there will be sport and play
and the Queen will be there.
Tristram gets excited when he hears this
and there is no chance he will miss out
on getting to her on the way,
and the day the King starts off
Sir Tristram comes into a bosky copse
where the road they will all take
goes through, do you see,
and he cuts off a hazel withy
and whittles it round with his knife,
and when the walking stick is done
he cuts his name on it
so when the Queen sees it
she will give it a Really Good Look.
(They have done this before,
so she will know it is him,
really really know it is him all right
when she sees the walking stick.)
And this is what he had Written To Her,
more or less:
He has stayed Away for quite a while
and waited and waited in banishment,
nosing around and trying to find out
how he could see her,
for he cannot live without her, cannot,

for Him and Her it is like
the Goatleaf vine
twining round the hazel tree,
ah, all wound round and holding on
tight to the trunk,
and they live like one thing, and live,
but if someone pulls them apart
the hazel dies straight away
and the Goatleaf on the same day exactly,
Darling Love, says Tristram, like Us.
No You without Me, no Me without You.
Now the Queen comes riding along
and looking round and everywhere,
and sees the walking stick, a Good Long Look,
and what is written on it, so she knows
and she orders the knights
riding along at the front
to stop stop stop she's getting off
to have a rest,
and they do what she says
and she walks off Away from everyone
and she calls her maid
Brenguin good and true and faithful,
and goes off the road a bit
and in the woods there she finds
The One Who Loves Her More Than Anything,
and oh what joy oh they are happy,
he can talk to her as long as he likes,
she can talk to him, Oh, my dear,
then she tells him all the things to do
to make friends with the King again
because he is sorry that he had to
send him Away
and he blames a bunch of slanderers
for it, then off she goes and leaves her love,
but when they part Oh God
they start crying and crying
and Tristram goes back to Wales again
until Uncle sends for him at last.
Now because of the jumping joy

he felt when he looked on his Love,
and because of what he had written,
which was exactly what the Queen said,
and to keep the exact words clear in his mind,
Tristram, who was a very good harp player,
made a bran new Lay out of it,
and the Name of it is easy enough to remember,
it is Goatleaf in English and
Honeysuckle in French,
and I have told it to you honestly and truly now,
just how it happened,
goodbye.

# and for Fröding

Gustaf Fröding was born in Alster (Värmland) in 1860. He spent much of his life in sanatoria, suffering from visions, disorders and alcoholism. His poems were greeted as 'dark, depressing syphilitic derangements', and he died in 1911 in Stockholm.

## Atlantis

Life's din streams from the city:
Big Music of the arch-strain struggle.
Now – then – like yells,
it slips from the bated falls…
out here it's quiet;
here the water lies
quiet in the still bay.

Here is deserted and still.
Here is far from that life.
Here dreams of dreams swim
woven round water and land.
Lean your head
here on my shoulder –
look over the shiprail.

Glimpsed things, there, at the bottom:
they are not rocks, reefs, skerries –
don't you see shining castles?
Can't you see palaces there?
Story-Atlantis,
Dream-Atlantis?
Don't you see the world that went under?

Gleamwhite walls
round a sheen Marbleburg,
rows of sacred statues,
gardens, squares, streets!
Empty now,
its sad recall
straggles through the city.

Gold-powered oppressors –
the rich men, ah, they, shrinking at Many,
stole the millions' happiness,
ate, drank, pleased –
the Victory of Taste –
and harder times,
harder the more they won.

And after great days
Atlantis the Strong sank and died:
the people, self-given to death,
lie in their graves,
glorious, bright,
sunk, slumped,
and come to ruin!

The sea has coral-decked
the dead-dream city
where the all-sleeping live.
Sunlight falls like dim star glitter
on grave calm.
Algae-twine
makes nets
around the colonnades.

It's coming, yes, for us too,
the sure, near hour of dying down;
it's coming, yes, for us too,
sleep and night,
wavemount
and wan sunlight
through it.

The city, dinning from land's end,
stands on its oozy clay ground.
Soon the sea will slip over the land,
over the cities.
Over us din,
over us pitch,
the people of a know-not race.


## Lovesong

I paid for my love:
the only way for me.
Sing sweet, rasp-strings,
keep singing sweet about love.

Dream that never came true;
lovely as a dream.
To me, shut out of Eden,
Eden is an Eden still.


## Sundown

Sat down on the mountain ridge,
looked out over the bay,
watched the west sun swim
far, far west wandering.
Time goes, goes,
just ago it was Spring,
soon Autumn will sheet the world.

Days have come, days have gone,
the last will come one day,
happiness littles in and clutters out,
hard to lose, so hard to lose.
Castles in the air
shimmer and call and smash.

Fool-folks think, fool-folks believe
fools plan and hope –
hope – wee sown grown seeds
that crop and bud up bright.
And new crops die,
frost nips and snuffs
what is planted in the earth.

# G is for Guglielminetti

Amalia Guglielminetti was born in Turin in 1891. She wrote in the plain style of the 'Twilight' school, and her poetry was thought to be mostly 'lonely and sad'. She died after an air raid in December 1941.


## Tomorrow

I feel tomorrow's shadow,
stuck, waiting, by my pillow,
with good and bad held in its hands.

Will bad be kept hid in the left?
Will good be kept hid in the right?
Which will be offered me? Which.

And sleep comes, down waving ways,
and buzzes to me – Don't worry, sleep now! –
and lays its finger softly on my eyes.

Sleep. Bitter hours may be fastened
in tomorrow's fist. Better not to worry.
Forget the shadow's silent spy that waits

to pounce, all ready, when you wake.

## Evening

And lone things love to linger now
beneath the alabaster sky
still bright with interrupting light.

See the shadows purple
the pallid mountains; and through the sky
the last lustre like a string ribbon.

Then a cloud obscuring all,
and on its edge, dismayed, alone,
the first star, like a quivered heart.

Single star, with bitter words
she tells you – I am like you! –
who troubles in the night

and cannot dare to tell you why.


## Stalker

There was someone hidden once
who followed me, close here, close there,
and tireless, with a quiet tread.

When darkness came, on some soft track,
I thought I felt it in my hair,
flutter-cringed and stooping.

Perhaps it was a bat; slight wings
that flit me with the anxious care
of tripping fingertips.

I doubted, and walked a little fearless faster,
but less demurely now,
and never sudden turned to see

what was there behind.

## Heart

I hear a heart down deep in its room,
the thumping, damped and hasty thuds.
You ask – is this my bumping heart or yours?

We listened. And it butted at its
coddled cell, debating in its care
the prisoned sparrow.

We listened with unknit souls
to the gentle, paired heartbeat
and asked – Is this my thudding heart or yours?

We listened. And the half-hid bumping fell
and faded in its lesser strength
so that we sighed, like those who still

forget to live – Is this my dying heart or yours?


## Happiness

And she who walks alone
still comes upon the shade of happiness
sometimes on her wandering way.

O it is a gentle shadow like
the Spring-dressed peace tree's,
its sourpink blossom-badges.

She is not sure if it was happiness,
and asks herself before the night
long looses all its black-flown hair:

O quiet voice that spoke to me,
(I like you) O perplexed smile,
O speechless and confessing hand,

were you happiness, or not?

## My Voice

My voice is not a sea-like roar,
or echoes high in columned lines,
but whispers like a rustling dress
that tells the end of women's trials.

I never cared to sing, but tried
to speak about myself, and women's
sleepless, wantful hearts, that leave
a little touch of bitters on the lips.

And bitter is my voice sometimes,
as if my quizzing laugh is shaking through,
and stings itself more than other ears.

And it is like a confidence of friends
that tells some secret sadness, and then fears
that they will laugh, and you will feel.

## and for Giusti

Giuseppe Giusti was born in Monsummarno Terme in 1809. He vigorously opposed Austrian rule, and 'surprisingly escaped the dungeons'. He became a member of the Tuscan Legislative Assembly, and died in 1850, in Florence, of TB.

### The Steam Chopper

In China there's
this steam-machine
that drives a guillotine.
In three hours it can shift
a hundred thousand heads in a row

                                    in one go.

Everyone's talking about it.
The Holy Thingummies can see
that the whole country
will be Civilised pretty soon,
and make Eurocrats

                       look like twats.

His Sublime Cloudiness is an honourable man:
a bit nasty, a bit tight,
a bit thick, but a real Benthamite,
and a Father to his People,
and happy to patronise whatever

                                 looks Arty or Clever.

Some dumb, ungrateful tribe of his
refused to pay
their Phase 2 Tax and Import Duty Section A,
so his Sublime Benevolence
sent the Thing to persuade

                           them. They paid.

The Chief Chopper is famous and rich,
with a Huge Pension
in honour of his invention
and Patent Payments and Prizes and Promotions,
and spends his time shopping
                              in Beijing.

The Holy Brothers here say they're keen
to get him baptised quick:
and the tinpot Duke of Modena says to his sidekick,
O O O why doesn't such
a super social pioneer
                    live round here!


## Mr Snail

Hooray for the Snail,
hooray for a horganism
that is admirable
and umble
and probably
gave the idea
of the Telescope
and the Winding Stair
to the astronomer
and the architect.
            Hooray for the Snail,
            dear little chap.

We might maybe call him
the Gastropodean Diogenes,
happy with the conveniences
God gave him.
He never leaves home
to go out:
he is safe and warm
in the little ways
of his own shell,
and never even gets the sniffles.
> Hooray for the Snail,
> dear little home-sweet-homer.

O let the tickle
of fantastical tucker
awaken the appetites
of duller tummies:
this one feels just fine
where he is
and loves to gnaw
tranquillillilly
the sweet, sprout grass
of his native land.
> Hooray for the Snail,
> dear little sober chap.

We all know the world is not
made out of kindness:
generally, it wants to be a lion,
not a donkey.
But the Snail,
contrarilarily,
knows when to put
his little horns away.
He is not pushy:
he sizzles, and is silent.
> Hooray for the Snail,
> dear little peacenik.

Nature, who teems with
all sorts of phenominations,
has blessed the Snail
Above All Others
because (listen, O
Chief Choppers)
he can even resurrect
his own head,
which is a miracle,
but true.
> Hooray for the Snail,
> dear little enviable chap.

O you wisest Owls
who preach
at your fellow men
and teach them nothing,
and you vultures,
fat pigs, birdbrains,
rabid would-bes
and clapped-out won't-bes,
let's all sing
the chorus please –
> Hooray for the Snail,
> dear little good example.

# H is for Hamoir

Irène Hamoir was born in Brussels in 1906. As a youngster, she was part of a family motorbike and car daredevil troupe ('the Leap of Death', 'the Infernal Tank'). She and her husband owned over one hundred Magritte paintings, and were stars of the artist's movie and painting sessions. She died in Brussels in 1994.


## The Highwiress

Deep in the river
I found pearl barley no
or seasoned seed no
but earth
earthfull
the sky's bare mouthful


One Sunday in 1926
I encountered
a red slab-ball of Dutch cheese
threaded with pearlings


Ye a.m. door sneak
scar-burned and ladder-burned
gnaw flour and soft wool
and the last salt o' the barn
wavy and warmish
the future opens its blue legs


Beneath the Great Wall of China
I pulled out my pistol
and the moon beam and the dew fall

In the metal water
a hibridged ship
horizon humpback


At last all the music is ssh
our teeth have unbolted our mouths
our throats squeezed our eyes scorched
tears oh clotty tears slidden from an overnude eye
do not enquire where they live
nothing of us invites anymore
now or after
thus I will close my complaint


Happy happy there who cares
king of the bowl
botheringnot the fish
tickled the public


My kind ill will gets me singing
the birds that sleep at my house
peck peck their seedies
I smooth their ploomage
they think I am wildrose
they open their too wings
poor dustbits in knotty fingers


The bedside light
oft
deceiveth
the bedside light
pokes out its tongue
wash
the beds I delight

She is one of those that tug my eyes
she is one of those who feign them unnoticed
she is not one of those that smile or quail
she is slender she is high she is blonde
her hair is a moony light
her face is a child drowned
her hands are bad dollies let loose
her wrists ivory bangles
I like the men who are with her
they are two they are skinny brown and sad
her dress is bright grey
the idiots know it not


This huge cadaver spread on the rails
knew the train times
it was ten o'clock
the next clatter would pass at midday


Towards Femminamorte in the Tuscan Apennines
he flummoxed forth full of fire
he had read in Manzoni
that She was in the graveyard
and had been for two hundred years


My lilylily my buttercup!
Do not await the frost!
My fount my life!
Do not wish for the frost
either

A very lovely lady in a romantic pinky dress with a selection of lacy skirts gallops through the dead town on a grey hoss. Just before the bridge a selection of people watch her go. They know that if she crosses the bridge and touches Alpha Tauri where it shines in the sky she will find happiness. She has just ridden across the bridge. Just past it is a great ditch. The hoss leapt so high it seemed ah to touch the star but fell plonk into the ditch crushing beneath her the madwoman in the lacy selection of skirts

Private person wishes to swap large wide life
for wallflower life

Beige sand Uhlan
in the hot sea breeze
naked under leather
place yourself thus in time
forget your hard arms
your soft eyes
forget the simple difficulties
and the long daysful
do not speak or dream
hear the near gulls scream

And she has lived greenly
that which greenfolks live

Some days in the year the sea parts itself with a dimsy divide
into two blocks of greyblue the surface of which raises itself
hither and thither lightlyslightly. Behind the strait of its unequal
masses done by their divide an unclean star reflectless. By the
edge of the sea there are black pebbles veined hither and thither
with white and crumblestones hand-size some of which resemble
fish heads have wavy lines on their flat tops.
The days I speak of the air is charged with a strange stuff that
colours it light brown darkcrazed.
This grey and this brown exhaust the eyes so one must find a
containment within. Fortunately there is always 'the farm'
unfortunately its people are dying of infant-tiles.


I have recently returned from England
I exchanged a grizzly for three indiarubbers
in Paris girls dance the Bug
in the chapel the cloakrooms flame in the sabbath night
Marceline, Gendarme, Carlyle, Byzantine
these raspberry boiled sweets come from Carpentras
the red has lied thrice
thrice he went to the Lama's mill


A window the windowpanes are filled with tears of rain
it is the bedroom of Mr Forgotten
Help! for the donkey is in the square
the sleepwalkers come in crowds
Help! they hang the year's white catkins from lanterns
Help! for the donkey is in the square
little girl little girl I shall often think of you


Here
Embeledo Garnero
served the Emperor

## and for Hofmannsthal

Hugo von Hofmannsthal was born in Vienna in 1874. Criticised as 'a weary alien with a nose for death', he was nominated three times for the Nobel Prize, but never won. He died, two days after the suicide of his son, in Rodaun, in 1929.

### The Emperor of China Says

At the Middle of Everything lives
Me, Heaven's Child.
My wives, my trees,
my animals, my pools,
are embraced by Wall Number One.
My Ancestors lie
in the Under-Palace,
honourably armed,
crowns on their heads,
all as they should be.
The steps of my Highness
boom down into the World's Heart.
Little rivers, exactly sent,
go east, west, north and south,
hushed out of my grass banks,
my green footpads,
to water my garden,
which is the Great Earth.
Here, they mirror the dark eyes
and coloured wings of my animals:
outside, they mirror coloured towns,
dark walls, thick woods,
and the faces of Many Men.
My Lords live round about me
like stars, and have Names
I have given them
to Honour the Hour

they came to my Presence,
wives that I gave them,
and their flocks of children:
for all Earth Lords
I have made eyes, shape, and lips,
like a gardener for his flowers.
But between the Further Walls
live my fighting people,
my field-farming people,
then More New Walls, and more,
and my Subject people,
the duller blood,
and down to the Last Wall, to the Sea,
that embraces my Lord-World, and me.


## Old Man's Summer Longing

When March is gone (good), and it's July,
just try and stop me – I'll be Out,
horse – car – train – maybe
I'll light on a lovely, hilly place;

big stands of serried trees,
planes – elms – maples – oaks – ah,
how long I haven't seen them. Maybe

I'll brake the horse, shout Stop
driver! and go all aimless off
deep in the summer country, on and on,

and maybe laze under these trees
with day and night together in their
tops – and not in this house

where days are blank with night,
and lightless nights creep like days –
and there, all life, and bright, and good.

And shadow-freed and evening-lit,
I light on happiness – a breath blown by
that whispers not 'This is all Nothing.'

The valley shades with lights
where houses are, and dark tops round me,
but the night wind does not say 'Death.'

I walk the graveyard, end to end,
and all I see is last-lit flowers,
and nothing else seems near to me.

Water burbles between dim turning
hazel bushes, and childlike I listen
and hear no whisper, 'What's the point.'

And quick, clothes off, I jump
in, and when I look long up
the risen moon is watching my splash.

Half standing in this cold cold swirl
I hurl an even stone way out to land:
and stand in moonlight.

And the shadow lies long along the moon-bright
summer land: this man, who dully
dreams aback this cushion by the wall.

Who sits so dully sad, half up, half down,
and glares at morning's striking light
and knows that something watches, waits for us.

The man maddened by the cross March wind,
the man that never gets to sleep at night,
black hands throttled round his heart.

O where is the summer land, and sweet July?

## Three Small Songs

I

Didn't you hear music
winding round the house?
In the hard, black night
who lay and played sweet-soft
on the hard stone: that was me.

I sang what I knew:
'Love, you are everything!'
Light broke out of the east,
day drove me hard home,
and my mouth is closed, closed.

II Green Song

The sky was cloudy-clogged.
We were alone, alone.
Broken each from each.
But not now.
The sky shifted, here, there,
and amidst it, all the world
shines like glass.

Risen stars lean,
glittering our cheeks,
and they know too:
their brightness brightens, brightens,
and we breathe want,
lying smile-surprised, feeling
your breath here, and mine.

III

The one-in-love said, 'I don't want you.
You have promised me nothing.
I don't want anyone.
People are not made to be true.

Go away. Travel, my friend.
Country and country and country.
Sleep in beds and beds.
Take this woman and that by the hand.

If the wine is too sour,
drink Malvasier.
If my mouth is sweet enough,
come back to me!'

# I is for Isanos

Magda Isanos was born in Iasi, Romania, in 1916. She survived polio at one and a half, but was left with poor health and a life-long limp. She believed that poetry should lean to 'the good, the generous and the beautiful'. Her health deteriorated, and she died in Bucharest in 1942.

## Sad Much

My heart is a pomegranate tree
full laden with bloody fruit;
I shook, but could not shake them down,
so you must come.

The branches try to reach
the sun and sky, unladen, straight,
you know their muchness hurts,
so pick them with your hands.

## Sing

I am like blind nightingales,
do I absorb the song, or does it me?
We rise so high sometimes…
my soul burns with a madcap flame.

My soul burns like God's–mouthed burning bush.
I believe in faery, saints and miracles;
my friends, make no wreaths for me.
My song in me is like the hush in you;
sometimes I sense it strong
but I know nothing, lowly I praise
the angel that has just come to my side.

Make me sing of people, sickness, whisper with cold lips made hot
about the poor, children, and their hunger.
And amidst my celestial terror
I see the fire-words I should use to make the world and put it back.

And then I am alone, and do not know, not now,
why God spoke from the burning bush to me.


## And We Die Like Tomorrow

It's sad to think one day,
perhaps tomorrow, all the wyndtrees
will be there, still bright,
and we will rot.

So much sun, God, so much sun,
will still be in the world that's after us;
whole litanies of seasons, rain
trickling cool from someone's hair…

The grass still grows,
the moon still bows amazed
above the streaming water,
but we will not be here a second time.

How strange that we can find
so sadly much time to hate
when life is just one drop
between this ticktock moment and

the next – how strange, how strange
and sad that we so little look
at the sky, pick flowers,
and smile, we
who all so quickly die.

## The Dress

Out of the moth and perfume trunk
my grandma took her young girl's dress.
Thin and light like smoke
as if woven out of air.

The silky crinoline swishy-sad,
its ruffles all undone and snicked,
and social silhouettes, instead of light,
dance in the room, called from their age.

And grandma sees her first dance,
remembers her beginner's dress,
and her hand shakes on cold satin,
quick with feeling.

Her head lower and still lower,
staring, stooping, the old shawl…
where is the beautiful dancer
that swirled in the party dress?

Little, light feet,
bright eyes, bright smile,
how did they fade forever
into grandma, and this hunch.

And the dead silk said,
(or maybe grandma did)
we are not dead, we dance on,
in other dresses, at our always-first party.


## Poem of the Sick Poet

I would happily part from my body,
where pain stalks me,
and come back in a fanspread of grass
and flowers in Spring.

How strange that God should need
this jar of blood,
unworthy and wayward,
when thoughts might mass maybe

on a butterfly wing,
or between roseleaves,
their shiver and drop so bright
on green grave beds.

Each time I feel this body, mouldered sick,
where my God sowed my soul,
I do not doubt His wisdom; but I think
that on the Sixth Day he was tired.


## A Vegetable Dream

I could be a tree,
growing by your window.
I could listen to you then,
and look at you all day,
and blossom in the winter
just to make you happy!
The pluffest birds would nest in my branches,
and nights give me earrings of stars
I would give you, like leaves.
Through the wide window often
I would sweetly lean down to kiss
the hair fallen on your face, or
your lips with mine, that are soft with flowers.
As Autumn comes I would toss apples
and redgold leaves for fun round your room,
keep your shutters from the rain, and,
perhaps, one moonlight night in Spring,
fairy folk will glide across the garden
and change me to a woman once again.
And then, damp with leaf and loam,
I would climb on your windowsill,
shimmer-faced with dew and moon,

and leap into your house: and quiet, calm,
unworded now for such a time,
and holding nests in either hand,
I would
start
to smile.

## and for Ioanid

Costache Ioanid was born in Bukovina in 1912. He said he wished only to serve God with his poetical gifts. His poem 'God Exists' is believed to have contributed directly to the downfall of the Ceaușescu regime. He died in Portland, Oregon in 1987.


### I'm Just…

I'm just a snowflake.
My exit is crystal-play.
A second is shook from all time,
smiles, drops, and other seconds enter.

I'm just a haywisp.
Mown with scythes and pitchfork-raked.
Earth stays and forgets it,
another wisp grows, dies so.

I'm just a pit-shadow.
But the star-trip is always open, always mine.
I'm not a marblefaced morning star,
but God is written on my brow.


### Swanchick

The first sunny day was sunning the woods,
woodpeckers beakily tapping the rosestocks
like smiley Spring tapping, tapping,
slight-fingered, on the World's Door.
The crofter climbed up her ladder
to put a little lid on the chimney,
and the mum-birds floffled in nests
hatching goldie chicks with beetroot beaks,
and, Right with the Laws of Life and Death,

a lovely chick popped out of each shell at the Right Time.
But out of one shell popped a chick
that was not lovely like all the others.
He did not have goldie feathers or glazebright wings.
He was smoky, with biiiiig saaaad eyes.
And all the other birds gawped at him,
and all the little fieldchicks pecked at him.
And his little neck bled,
and he couldn't find any friends.
And at night, when all the little chicks went to snuggle
under warm wings and soft love-touches,
he pattered up along with them, shyly, for a sleep,
to hush his poor little body and soul,
but he did not get peace and soft love-touches,
just smacks that made him flap-patter away.
He shivered in the shadows, droopy, staring
at the nest like it was a castle in a magic meadow,
and nodding off on the ladder where he perched,
all afraid of Bad Animals, and softly saying,
Why don't you love me, mum?

Ah, but on the water, while all the other clutchy-claw chicks
gawped lakewards from the bushy shadows,
the Ugly Chick paddled perfectly,
which made the others all wonder and ashamed.
And he glided on to the pinkpink horizon
through the wind-wavy lakeweeds
to heal his little soul's hurt.
And sometimes, in the evenings, paddling late
amongst the stars, he thought he saw soaring glitters,
and then voices, coming closer and closer…
then swishing away into the ruby-barred sky.
And the voices seemed to call to him and
ah how sweet they sounded! And sometimes, all lonely,
in his little secret in-me voice he would suddenly shout Mum!
and his eyes would search the sky…

So the lonely days and nights went by
and the goldie chicks grew up,
squawky-scrapping about, flopping in the sun

like strings of shiny coloured beads,
and the little unBrave, no-friend chick
got uglier, and smokier, and lonelier.

But then came Autumn, and the wind wobbled the coast trees,
and a strange magic came too.
His smokygrey feathers went white,
his neck turned into a snow-white harp
like lilies, and lilies all wreathed his shoulders,
and he set off on the water without looking back,
and paddled far away in the peaceful peace,
and paddled all night, far, far away.
And when the sun came up, all of a sudden he saw
a white star-cloud streaming on the horizon.
And with a little cry and a tear, the chick
lightly spread his lilywhite wings
and took off over the water, stroking air,
towards the white swans flying, flying, calling, calling.

And nothing in the crofter-valley knew
that the mumless, cuddleless chick
soared, like a miracle, through dark to the bright bird-cloud,
and vanished in a deathless Spring dawn.

## Whoever Loves a Flower

Whoever loves a flower
is near a holy hiddenness.
Whoever stops on the road
to hear the sound of Spring
is near
near Heaven…

Whoever loves bright sky,
when the sun floats into blue,
whoever breathes wonder
when it burns red in the sea
is near
near Heaven…

Whoever stares at bare granite
in the purple mountains,
whoever threads wild maple woods
on lone men's tracks
is near
near Heaven...

And the man who has mercy
from the sweet Lamb's hurts
is the flower's brother,
the river's, the mountain's, the sea's,
and wherever his track goes
all Heaven
all Heaven is in him.


## Just the Thought

Just the thought of You makes me hope
on my Heaven-tending way.
Just the longing for You and Your grace-full face
tells me all the time...
soon...
soon...

One day I'll stand by the castle gate
far, far off in Your country.
I stay awake, I startle
with this heartflamed want,
and wait for You...
and wait for You...


Just this world's wanderer,
I clamber to the stars on a thrill-ladder.
With every sparkle I gasp and want:
O please come...
sooner...
sooner...

## Like Dew Goes

Like dew goes,
lapped by lilies,
like clouds go
and others come,
like sound scatters
on windy wings,
everything in the world
passes.

The more you collect,
the more you save,
the more name you want,
the more show you keep,
the more you get
what you want,
the harder it is
to go.

The fever and the fire,
the famous life,
they all have their way
and their end.
We will all go
and leave what we had:
some quiet,
others sad.

# J is for Jórunn

Jórunn skáldmær was born in Norway in the first half of the tenth century. The fragments here, part of a long poem called *Sendibítr*, are preserved in the writings of Snorri.


## The Bite Letters

1
this king gored clasht-blades
in cursed men's blood
their troop fell at his fury
and fire felled every toft

2
it seems Halfdan that Harald Lighthair
has heard of these rougheries
but the poem lies still dim deep
to this blade-basher

3
and the great kin King of war
geared up to crow
when his quick killers scuttled
to bathe their blood-reeds in the scab-sea

4
where in the world are two Lords likelier
to hear of their own high honour
won at the arrow-hail
given to these dreamless deathmen
given by hard-headed land Kings
because of bright Sindri's blessing
the lives of Lords were lifted

5

the goldring giver sang
a mighty song for Harald
Guthorm got his poem-pay
from the listening King
and this tree of war ended thus
the high Kings' highest quarrel
which had nudged them to ready
their armies all for the storm of swords

# and for Jacobsen

Jens Peter Jacobsen was born in Jutland in 1847. He wrote poems, novels (admired by Rilke), and short stories, and translated Darwin's *Origin of Species*. His most famous novel was *Niels Lyhne* (much admired by T.E. Lawrence). He died of TB in 1885.

## A Landscape

Ssh, my love:
we must walk quiet together.
There's a song asleep here,
in the woods' night's hush.

Waves and wind are quiet,
the songbirds' songs are still,
small streams whisper gleamy
through the mossy ground.

Moonbeams shift
silent at the beech trees,
a white edge dreams away
down the quiet paths.

One silvery cloud above
rests on a wide-laid wing,
and high through the treetops
it looks, and listens.

Waves and wind are quiet,
we must walk quiet together.
There's a song asleep here
in the woods' night's hush.

## Evening Time

The sun's last line of light goes out
and dark night is born;
each flower eye silent shuts,
bent at the swollen ground,
and the sky's wept water thickens
on the world of the day's light flood.

The birds fall something-still,
less happy and less song;
Spring breaks with a sob
from the dark hid hall,
and pours ink twilight like
funeral stuff across the fields.

In the trees a sigh
just born in the new wind's breath,
and the heart of the sea swells
with leaden waves;
ah, the sun's last light has gone,
and bright day is dead.


## Spring Can Come When it Wants

Spring can come when it wants,
with greenest greening,
with a thousand birds' flute-games,
while flowers flower
and all that is beautifullest,
glory and glorious,
comes and flutters
out on the pasture, out on the fields,
gushing in gardens and hooded in woods,
splashes its scent on fields and water.
What do they do to me?
My heart is not a flower, nor a leaf.
Spring does not make it smile.
It has its own, strange Spring.
When?

## Autumn

The forest is wearing its regallest robe,
fruit has filled the leaves with splendour,
there is no room for more richness,
not an inch between now and its purpose,
the purpose is here.

The harvest wind curls and kisses, baleful
and sly, each leaf on its twig,
*remember the warm Spring wind*
*when you were young,* cold nudge of the time
when green was the purpose.

Each leaf thinking thinks of
the season when smiling it dreamed as its bud,
the second when, set free, it stretched
at the light that had dandled it out
and touched it green.

It wants that time again,
when it fluttered fresh in the wind;
but has not found the new sweet colour of Spring,
hangs dry and greenless,
and the purpose is here.

The harvest wind curls and yells, savagely
striding the leaves, its sniggered song:
*you are doddery-old, too old,*
*and will fall, all fall from your branches;*
*the purpose is here.*

And the leaves all fall. But some small,
like buds again,
still curl, torn from their twigs,
to hold in their dreams at the end
the purpose of Spring.

## In a Seraglio Garden

Roses swag their heads, heavy
with dewdrip and scent,
and stone pines nod so, hushed and flat
in muggy air.
Fountains wheel their silver spouts
in drowsy lines,
minarets point their turk-towers
up into Heaven,
and the crescent moon drifts its glazy pathway
over the glazy blueness,
and kisses rose and lily masses,
and all the far, small flowers
in the seraglio garden,
in the seraglio garden.


## Silk Shoe Fitted on a Gold Last

Silk shoe fitted on a gold last!
I've got a girl for sure!
I've got a gorgeous girl for sure!
There's no one like her in all God's sunny world,
no one so only-one.
She's as pure as the south sky,
as the north snow.
There is earth's delight in my Heaven,
and flames zoom out of my snow.
No summer rose is redder
than her black eyes are black...

# K is for Konopnicka

Maria Konopnicka was born in Suwałki in 1842. She wrote poems, short stories, children's books, newspaper articles and criticism, and translated Heine, Rostand and D'Annunzio. She travelled much in Western Europe, concerning herself with the independence of Poland, women's rights and the plight of the poor. She died in Lviv in 1910.


## I Know That In Your Small Window

I know that in your small window I will not see
a light lit by your hand…
I know that somewhere there is a shivered, ravelled
echo, woken by your troubled song…
I know that on this white and silent wall
no fitful shadow of you will come or go…
but still I keep my rapt eyes
upon your empty, lonely house.


## I Say: Go Away! – But Come Back, Silent…

I say: go away! – but come back, silent,
to look just once again where your feet trod,
and I listen to the wind, breathing far away,
and look at the pale and fading flower.
It is a flower that has a soul –
and I don't know where I am – and weep.

I say: stay! – and go away myself,
and wander, shorn, in the dark.
And I feel the briars prick as I pass,
and hear the heart's burial bells.
And I see the darkling graves of people's dreams –
and I don't know where I am – and can't go on.

Two ways – but still one longing,
two ways – but one disquiet.
One way I see the golden sunrise fade,
one way the sorrow-shadowed night draws near...
It is late – the dew falls,
and I don't know where I am – pallid and becalmed...

# and for Kapnist

Vasily Kapnist was born in the Ukraine (Obukhovka) in 1758. Anti-serf, anti-official, and an enthusiast for the simple life, he was briefly sent to Siberia. 'Vulgar, common and scurrilously liberal', Kapnist translated 'Ossian', Horace and the Biblical Psalms. He died in Obukhovka, and is buried by the river there.

## Storm Coming

Dark thrown on the sun,
like curdled smokeblack.
The bright sky palled
with a dim night winding–sheet.
Storm coming. Wailing wind.
The roused woods clamour,
the crackgust blow swarms on the harvest,
a hum that threatens mounts far off.

Quick, into the haycock,
and down with the golden sheaves.
Now, now the rainspout cuts down
into the valley jaws.
The wind has sown
your corn with hail
across the fields and blackthorn grove,
and strewn the land's sweet favour.

Too late, too late for you now
to make and mend in its ill wind,
when rain sheets from the loomed storm sky,
and pours rivers down the fields.
Quick, take your children
and run to your village:
save yourself there.
Listen. Near. A thunderclap.

## Silhouette

Your likeness clearly chased inside me –
why do you give me this shadow?
To make some grey friend
of my vivid love?
Can love's arrow be ripped from a heart?
Ah, only the death of blood and life will kill
this circulatory fire.

Take it back. Blank present.
Ah, no. Let it stay. Still.
I'm happy enough in my black, wrongwent way.
Let me fool myself with sugared hope,
staring staring at your loved like-lines –
when like your shadow held in them,
a small shade of love is kept in you.


## Sigh

Late one day, in the cool of a slight wood,
Milena and I watched two doves
dancing with themselves.
My passion gingered,
my soul on my tongue – but,
ah, heart-full, I shied,
and words dwindled on a sigh.
And why did my lips only hush
with my secret still hidden and dumb?
If you wanted that secret, sure
you could find it plain in the sigh.
Must we always and ever, so often unright,
say promise my love is certain and here?
The eyes of the soul should see all,
and the heart send word to the heart.

## A Poor Man's Riches

The fat smiling men of this world,
struttant and glorious-vain,
have only Themselves
in their General View.
But I will make do
with peace with you,
and happy in this but&ben,
unblown with puff.

Let dealers raven
the sea for gold;
let princes splosh waves of blood
for one step of somebody's land.
But I will make do
without the blood-bought world,
richer than princes
just with your love.

The but&ben is plain;
with you it is Holy Walls;
and all I ask God for here
is the peace and quiet of us.
And I will make do with my life
and ask for no longer:
I am only afraid, my friend,
to leave and outlive you alone.

# L is for Lasker-Schüler

Else Lasker-Schüler was born in Elberfeld in 1869. She lived in Berlin as a 'bohemian' writer until the Nazis came to power, when she went to live in Jerusalem. Usually called an Expressionist, she wrote poems and plays concerning matters of love and religion. She died in 1945.

## Homesick

I cannot talk the language
of this keen country,
or walk its unlike walk.

Or even unpuzzle
the passing clouds.

Night is a Stepmother Queen.
I think of the Pharaoh's forests, think
and kiss mere pictures of my stars.

Now my lips glisten,
and talk of Far and Gone,

And I am a picturebook,
motley in your lap.

But your face weaves
a blind of tears.

The corals of my glittered birds
are all prised out

and on the garden hedges
their soft nests turn to stone.

Who will hallow now my dead halls –
they bore my father-crowns,
whose prayers sank in the sacred river.


## From Afar

Your heart is a brightling night.
I see it –
you are thinking of me – all the stars stop.

And your body like the gold moon
so quickly gone
shining from afar.


## A Hush of Words

You took the stars
from over my heart.

My shrivelled thoughts,
I must dance.

And look up, up, at whatever you do,
and wear my life.

I cannot lift the evening
over the hedges any more.

In the mirror of the creek
I cannot find my own reflection now.

You have robbed the Archangel's
floating eyes.

Yet I sip the syrup
of their blue.

My heart sinks slow –
to somewhere, somewhere –

perhaps into your hand.
That touch-insists at all of what I am.


## My Lovesong

My blood mutters
like a hidden spring,
always you, always me.

My bare and hunting dreams
dance beneath the giddied moon,
sleepwalk children,
soft across dark hedgerows.

Ah, your lips are sun…
heady scents, your lips…
and out of silver-circled catkins
you laugh… you, you.

And a snaking trickle
always along my skin,
my shoulder, on and over –
and I listen…

My blood mutters
like a hidden spring.


## World End

There is a keening in the world,
as if great God were dead,
and the lead shadow and the downfall
press, grave-laden.

Come, for we want to hide more hidden...
life lies in all hearts
as if in coffins.

And you! We want to kiss more deeply –
longing raps upon the world,
and we must die of it.

(for H.W. in memory of many years)


## The Three of Us

Our souls hung on morning dreams
like sweet cherries,
like bright tree blossom.

Our souls were children
when they played with life
like fairy tales.

And late summer skies sang
of the white homesick-bush
above us, in the fluttered southern wind.

And a kiss, and a believing
made our souls,
we three doves.


## My People

The rock that bore me,
where I sing my God songs,
turns brittle...
Suddenly, I stumble from the track
and crumble all into myself
far off, alone above the dirgeing stone,
towards the sea.

My blood's fermenting
flows all away,
away and out.
And always, always still the echo
in me,
when in terror at the East,
the brittle cliff,
my people
screamed to God.

# and for Laforgue

Jules Laforgue was born in 1860, in Montevideo. 'Symbolist, impressionist, self-pitying, bored and hysterical', according to opponents, he 'invented' *vers libre*, and died, obsessed with loneliness and mortality, in poverty, of TB in Paris, 1887.

## Night Poem

Day, dying; worn sun; and I think…
gasp, panic, butting fingers at my forehead,
and yet, over there, three chattery girls
stitch in the hushlight of a lamp.

## The Night I Heard a Lost Dog

I shall always hear that bark. There.
A rawbone dog lost in endless lands
where mad clouds bolt in a drab
rain sky, and night yowls on and on.

Ah, no one cares to cry for History's hurts.
Sleep, sing, love, oh unmemoried men,
but your turn will come – blank, the black ditch.

Did you hear? Huh? That pitiful howl.
It's the sad, lonely squeal and grate
of a black, damned, rite-wrung pilgrim train
in a dirgy night, plunging on, on.

Ah, no one cares to cry for History's hurts.
Sleep, sing, love, oh unmemoried men,
but your turn will come – blank, the black ditch.

Oh the gnawing song again I hear at night:
a dance, flowers, glasses, fulldress, lights.
The wind laughs in the pinetrees that billow beer
to the face-cake couples who hoof it today.

Ah, no one cared to cry for History's hurts.
In a hundred years you will be all black-ditched,
far from the resung dance of the unmemoried men.


**Doubtful Christmas**

Christmas! Christmas! I hear the night bells...
and I have put down my pen on these unfaithful pages:
sing! O memories! All my show turns tail
and I feel myself in my great gall again.

Ah! these night voices that sing Christmas! Christmas!
carry me out of the up-twinkling nave
a home truth so soft, so mother-sweet,
that my overblown heart blows up in my chest...

And I listen to these night bells, on and on...
I'm the freak of the human family,
and the wind carries me in its nasty fastness
the prickling witter of a far-off rejoicing.


**Nightmare**

Through the backward dumps of a weedy, weeping organ
carriages, papers, yelling advertisements,
go the passers-by, iced up, bashing carelessly,
flower sellers with their bad-try pregnancies...

Along the golden cafés where withered youths
stare in their absinthes, idiot-eyed,
file the huntress troop of old paint-faces
pricing their hag-ridden houri bait.

And Jesus and Buddha have gone! And history blares
for a Witness! Everything is alone. In the splendour
of fair far suns, no immortal eye –

everything is stupid and still soon gone, soon gone.
What stuff! O God! Madness. Is it possible.
When will we see the end of this vast nightmare.


**April Wait**

Must be midnight. Five to. Everyone is sleeping.
Each man picks his flower from the green dream garden,
and I, tired of taking my old, peaceless shame,
rack my heart for the drip drip drip of golden rhymes.

And then, by mindfuls, a chord comes back to me,
a stupid tune from long ago – and you rise, soundless,
O minuet, brighter than ever, from those gone hours
when I was green and good, sweet and still to be believed.

And I put down my pen. And I dug in the innocent,
loving, now and forever impured life –
and I stay, and I stay, elbows on the page,

lost in the why of worldly things,
listening dully in the lonely night
to the foul clatter of an old, late-out carriage.

## M is for Maksimović

Desanka Maksimović was born in Rabrovica in 1898. She taught in various schools and colleges for most of her life. Her poetry has been called 'the best use of the Serbian language', as well as 'patriotic, and full of love'. She died in Belgrade in 1993.

### Hand

Weight, all bony knuckles,
an old hand lies in a lap.
Bluebranch veins,
tangled alphabet of wrinkles
patterned there.

But when it lifts to a child's head
it lightens and lives,
like a watered plant,
bane and tiredness tapped from the veins,
knucklebones knit,
a joint nursed in another.
But when the child is gone
the hand goes drear again,
and ebbs to the lap,
like a grave.

### To Never Pilgrims

To you who have never
been pilgrims,
have never lit a flame
with their own hands,
or roused spark from stone,
who have not help-sprung water from a rock,
or made a hut of mud,

or straw,
who have not rafted down a flood,
or broken ships,
who have not journeyed
with an ant alone for a friend,
you who have not been alone
with some great stretch
of sea, with hope, despair,
who do not know the first floor
of the universe,
who have not lived a day alone and long
in star-pricked steeps
or warmed themselves
with poet-pilgrim ecstasy.


## Brachisland Pine

Pine tree branches
breeze above me,
a ride of ravens on them,
turned stone still.
Or maybe swallows' nests
or wasps',
or iconlamps soot-coated.

Lying here since morning, palely waiting:
will the birds there flap down,
will I hear the wasps' whine,
or maybe the iconlamps alight?

Evening comes, the north wind too,
with mad unquiet,
winding down delusions from the tree,
and there they changed
in sudden, strange surprise – to pinecones.

## Come to the Woods

Come to the woods with me,
where I watch tonight
pale autumn
flower and fall
on the small, flat tracks.
Come to the woods with me,
where we watch each pool
peer a yellow moon.

Come to the old,
deep woods:
where weary oak limbs
fall silently tonight.
Come to the woods,
where all about
piles of dwindled springs
smell sad.

Come through the bitter
thicket grin:
where grand white beech-stands,
elm-shades look
softly blue tonight.
Come to the woods,
where pines hold heaven
over our heads as we go.

Come to the woods,
where on streams tonight
silver is hushly strewn.
Come to the woods,
where under the stars
sere leaves dream in calm
on paths and brigs,
hill-span, dale-spread.
Come to the woods,
remember me unquietly tonight
and always.

# and for Maeterlinck

Maurice Maeterlinck was born in Ghent in 1862. A simple and strong man hiding behind a mask of fashionable decadence, he enjoyed bee-keeping, smoking, beer, cycling, skating, woodwork, cars and canoeing. He wrote for exactly two hours a day. He died in Nice in 1949.


## Dead Hours

Old passions passing,
more worn men's thinking dreams,
more wearing sleeping dreams;
days of hope passing!
Which one should I run from today?
No more stars, no more,
just iced dullness
and blue rags across the moon.
More caught trapped sobs and
there, fireless sick men,
and lambs cropping at snow:
my God, have pity on it all!
I wait for some stirring,
I wait for sleep to pass,
I wait for a little sun
on my moon–iced hands!


## Nightsoul

Now, at the end, my soul is sad;
tired of its tiredness,
weary of its waste,
sad, tired, weary,
and I wait for your hands on my face.

I wait for your clear fingers on my face,
like frosted angels,
I wait for them, with their ring,
I wait for their coolness on my face,
like some sea-sunk richness.

I wait, at the end, for their cure,
so I do not die in sunshine,
I wait for them to clear my half-warm eyes,
where so many thin, tired things sleep!

Where so many swans on the sea,
swans straying on the sea,
put up their hopeless necks!
Where sick men pick roses
in winter gardens!

I wait for your clear fingers on my face,
like frosted angels,
I wait for them, lapping my sight,
the dead grass of my sight,
where so many tired lambs straggle.


## Tired Beasts

O far gone passions,
laughs and sobs!
Sick and half eye-shut
in the leafless leaves,

my sins' yellow dog,
my hates' squint hyena,
and lions of love couched
on the wan, dull plains!

In their unable dream,
dull under their dull,
drear and faded sky
they stare… stare…

at temptation's sheep,
that space away slowly, one by one,
in the moveless moonlight –
my still-stood passions!


## Reflections

My soul frights, my soul frights
under hoisting dream water.
And the moon lights in my heart
that has dived in the dream spring.

Only the deep reflection of things
still cries in the water deep,
lilies, palmleaves, roses,
under the reeds' bored stillness.

Flowers drop petal and petal
on the sky reflection above,
falling, now and forever,
under dream water and the moon.

# N is for Noailles

The Princess Anna Elisabeth Bibesco-Bassaraba de Brancovan (Anna de Noailles) was born in Paris in 1876. Successful, rich, and famous, she published much poetry, which was thought 'rather gushing'. Friends with Proust, Gide, Colette and Cocteau, she was the first woman to be awarded the Legion of Honour, and the brightest light of high society before the First World War. She died in 1933.

## You Are Like Music

You are like music:
that eye of hurt,
that hearking wander
of your small and weary smile;
the longingest songs
that lap my heart blood
have no fiercer force
than your frailty and pallor.
Church lights
shine thus,
as your face, where I, too deep,
have drunk at a new Host.

You are only a faint child,
but in my heart's dreams
you are like War,
like Jesus midst the Doctors,
like heroes dead beneath ramparts,
like the tremble and struggle of everything,
like The Cid on a dancing horse,
like the killed of the Coliseum
on whom the ramping beast
rolls, like a soothest sheet
all logged with love and blood,
his peace and drowsy tongue.

## I Slept, I Wake...

I slept, I wake, and feel my sorrow.
Reslamming pain bursts in me
like gunshot fired in my heart.
A minute's sleep is a feeble scarp
against my Fate, so sure and strong.
Shall I never again see your brother-eyes?
Never again hear your warm words?
Ah! Are there such goodbyes that are not Death?
What speaks? My body and my thoughts are waste.
My dear familiar room is strange;
has my mind gone out?
A great great sadness is not clear so soon;
I try, but can I bear this weight?
What quiets, what journeys
if I never see the seeming of your face?
My mind, a bitter grey forever,
holds a dead world, and devastated stars.
I know no more, my life so bled,
be it you or the world that has gone.
And even in dreaming, in thoughts more plain,
I argue still with myself, so I do not leave you...

## Bells of Venice

Beggary, hunger, the sun's great load,
the killing labour of this aged child,
who breathes and weaves the reek of basil and honeyed oil
about the yellow and the silver-gilded couches.

The foetid crawl of drowsed canals,
the mouldered house hung with washing,
fevers and thirst, that I would rather choose
than not to hold your hot and living hand.

Upon the hour when Venice bells,
out-breathing like a fervid sigh, strew into the plain air
that voluptuous cry of passion and alarm:
'Enjoy, enjoy the passing time!'

# Palermo Adrowse

Palermo slept: the Tyrrhenian Sea
loosed its sour and sea-kine smell:
smell of algae, urchins, salt and coral,
smell of the sea where sirens die;
that smell, swimming in the warm seaspray,
so swell with bold, vast violence,
that it seemed a bitter, thrilling charge
upon the sleeping earth, near scentless-numb…

Signatures of blessing seemed to fall from the palms;
the little boats passed on to fish for tuna;
and I watched, my forehead bathed in still mists,
the face of Heaven Plato looked upon.
There, at the darkling terrace edge, rose the sound
of a voice exhausted by heat;
each murmured word seemed soft as confidence;
one long sigh usurping the air:
and the wind, gasping like a hunted bird,
fled towards the sky in sprays of coolness…

Digging at darkness, grinding the pebble road,
the idle coach we sat in
plunged into the thick and twining night,
under the careless, immutable, clear sky;
it was the hour when the cooled air subtly enters
the massy stone of quiet monuments;
in these divine moments, cloaked in shadow,
I found no happiness – yet hoped to,
for happiness is only a presentiment:
a taste before itself, and never truly known…

In a deep garden running by our road,
cats, mind-troubled in this smooth season,
launched their burning howls of slaves and masters.
Upon the folding piles of jasmine and carnation
we heard them moan their fiery call,
like cruel doves in fierce fight…
and then the silence once again, indolent and heavy;

our coach through the open darkness.
I thought of the past; waves on the sand
again, again, always again, with calm measure,
laying down their burden of murmurs and smells...
the stars, with secret gazing, pinned
to their sublime dome, swarming, thronging,
drew sighs from eyes that looked upwards...
and the room of nights rang
with the silent cry that swelled in my dreams!

# and for Nerval

Gérard de Nerval was born in Paris in 1808. He lived a life of poetry, nervous breakdowns and insanity. He took his pet lobster for walks in public gardens. When friends found him dreaming, they feared to wake him, lest he fall from 'the great heights of his imagination'. He hanged himself in Paris in 1855.

*Eight Odelettes*

## Lords and Flunkeys

Those long-gone lords out of novels,
those big beefheads, things out of Dante,
with giant bonehouse bodies
that could have come rootstocking out of the earth –

if they came back to the world, and decided
to inspect the heirs of their Deathless Names,
that tribe of Laridons that clutter the Cabinet
Villas, grovelling, greedy and cheap;

spindly, corseted things, stuffed shirt-fronts, fake pad-legs –
surely these lords would know that, since
long ago their girlies had souped
flunkey blood with the lordly kind.

## Waking Up in a Carriage

Here's what I saw – trees jumble scramming
down the road like a routed army;
under me, like it was pitched by the whip wind,
the ground, bowling in torrents of clumps and cobbles.

In the green plains belltowers led
their villages of tile-topped plaster houses,
that trotted after like a flock
of white sheep, black-stamped red.

And the drunk mountains ricketed; the river,
outrolled on all the valley like a boa snake,
struck out to cramp them in…
and I was… I was just waking up in the postcoach.


## Change

So you stop travelling, get down from the carriage,
and wander, intendless, between two houses,
headspun with the horses, the road, the whips,
eye-droopy and drowsy all over –

And then, there, suddenly, green and hushed,
a damp valley lapped in lilacs,
a creek rustling between poplars –
and the road and the row are quickly forgotten.

So you lie in the grass and listen to you living,
and slowly get drunk on the smell of hay,
and stare at the sky all thoughtless…
then, oh well, someone yells, 'Time to go, folks!'


## Luxembourg Street

The girl's gone,
quick, busy as a bird,
holding a glossy flower,
singing some new song.

Maybe she's the only girl in the world
whose heart would fit mine,
who would light up my deep, dark night
with one look.

No, no – my youth is gone…
the soft beam that glowed me –
scent, girl, tune…
good times go – they are gone.


## Notre-Dame

Notre-Dame is old, old, old. Maybe one day
she'll bury the Paris she watched being born.
But, some century, time will haul this
lumped carcass down, like a wolf hauls down a bull,
bend her iron nerves and gnaw, gnaw
her old rock-bones with deaf teeth.

People and people from all round the world
will come and study this stark wreck
and wonder, reading the Hugo-Book…
 – and they'll think they can see the old church
like it was, splendid strong, ramped
in front of them like a dead thing's shadow.


## April

Fine days already, dust,
blue burning sky,
red burning walls, long days,
no green: slowly, slowly,
a reddy glare works
the great, black branched trees.

Fine days clog me, and bore me.
Only after rain
should Spring appear,
in an act in green and pink,
played by a cool girl
smile-stepping out of the water.

## Imagine

There's a tune that I'd give
all of Rossini for, and Mozart, and Weber –
an old, old tune, sluggish sad,
with secret charms just for me.

And every time I hear it,
my soul reyoungs two hundred years:
it's Louis the Thirteenth Time... I see a green
hillside laid yellow in the setting sun.

And a brick castle with stone corners,
windowpanes stained red,
lapped in vast parkland, feet steeped
in a river flowing amongst flowers.

And a woman at a tall window,
yellow hair, black eyes, in clothes-gone-by...
who I've seen before, maybe,
in another life... and I remember.


## Grandmother

My grandmother died three years ago.
A good woman. And when she was buried
parents, friends, everyone cried,
truly, bitterly, sadly.

But I roamed the house more surprised
than sad; and when I went near
her coffin – someone asked how
I could look at her silent and tearless.

Noisy sorrow passes quickly.
After three years, other feelings,
good, bad, revolutions,
have wiped this memory from people's hearts.

But I think of it, and often cry.
After three years, catching strength from time,
like a name scored in tree bark,
her memory cuts deeper into me.

# O is for Otto-Peters

Louise Otto-Peters was born in Meissen in 1819. Generally regarded as the forerunner of German women's rights, she wrote tirelessly for journals and newspapers, and founded magazines and movements, recruiting women for the 'Land of Freedom'. She died in Leipzig in 1895.


## At My Husband's Grave

Your picture occupies my heart,
your name re-echoes through my songs,
in spite of death and parting I draw gently near
your grave with love again:
even the shrill discord of death will never
break the sweet harmony of two souls.


## Swallows

Once with happy songs
the swallows came,
and now they fly away
in kept and dreadful silence.

But surely that is good:
they have brought songs
that stay with us,
and so they sing no more.

But we can sing
still again in ice and snow –
the swallows fly mute,
but thanks – Godspeed, Godspeed!

## Easter Holiday

In the hush of Sunday morning a brass fanfare
clangs from the church tower: God is risen!
He lies no more in guttered winding sheets;
it seemed the sky flared purple.

Slowly it seemed to splatter sparks,
larks churred up their happy hoots,
gold-drops lit in the violet's eye,
and each bud dreamed that it had blown.

Such revels urge the anxious heart
to start again the blossomed gleam and sun
of some new smiling life.

The grave, the cross and all great pain
are overthrown by Heaven's power.
Victory peals out, and happily we weep.

## Fog

A grey veil crowds all about –
will the sun see through? How can I know.
Will fog unface her fully all the day?
And if she comes, or if she sets?
How can I see – as all the earth slumps quietly,
and field and combe fill up with mist.

The wood, a vapoured altar, steams,
and one wary eagle circles all alone
with want to slip up sunwards –
but here today is only some dun spot
amidst a sea of air, consumed with grey.
And silence anxious-strange.

A picture of our time. Shut in with fog –
no sweeping storm, no gleaming sun –
the Earth in one wide-wrapping cloud!
No eagle's eye can find the sunlight glow,
the freedom-sun is masked to death –
a muffled quiet all the country round.

# and for the Olafssons

Pall Olafsson was born in 1827 in east Iceland. He had no schooling, became a farmer, clergyman and poet, and died in 1905.

Jon Olafsson, his brother, was born in 1850, and left Danish-controlled Iceland at 22 for America. On his return he became a Member of the Icelandic Parliament. He wrote all his poems for one woman, whom he loved for forty years, and eventually married.

*Pall Olafsson*

### Hello Summer!

Thanks, Summer sun!
Gold-wrapping hills and straths,
gold-holding skyhigh pikes
and blue moor lakes:
falls, creeks, rippled rivers,
happied in your golden hair:
and your warm wisp
on the white glacier's drop.

And gold-shine clothes for everything!
You quicken hope in men:
your blink kisses them.
Birds toot in the glens,
you make the day less dreary-long
and usher, usher to our country crofts
the warm south breeze.

You spawn, smile, stock and sheet
highlands and hollows!
And when you set,
everything sorrows in the cold.
Thanks, Summer sun:

gold-wrapping hills and straths,
gold-holding skyhigh pikes
and blue moor lakes!


*Jon Olafsson*

## My Kingdom

Clouds drag up and murk the world,
things look bitter and black:
but I'm in my well-met, mighty kingdom –
the fair, clear, sun-skied Land of Dreams.

Spring is slow, oaks slow leafing,
the pasty fields green slowly:
but Spring is forever and ever-green
in the sun-become kingdom of Dreamland.

Longing for my homeland, always longing,
mad to see what I can't see... white mountaintops:
but I have a Dreamland that is better,
ah, better even than Iceland.

They can judge me, and put me in prison,
pack me out of my family land:
but this is a free place, a perfect Dreamland
that is always waiting for me.

I left family, friends, left to be
this lonely stranger in a new country:
but my soul is still living with them
in its Land of Dreams.

Some friends, old friends I loved,
are gone, icecold in their grave-dark:
but I can still see them, be near them,
in Dreamland's sun-bright thoughts.

So what if I'm poor, always have been,
not given this day my daily bread:
there are gold times on the sparkled sand
in the sweet wish-thoughts of Dreamland.

Remember! The high thrones of the great
kings of the world all tumble:
but why would I care which way their kingdoms go?
Mine is the Land of Dreams.

The fiery-sore hurt of my mind's pains
brings tearfuls for family, friends:
but Dreamland's smiles, smiles of its hopeful sun,
kiss them off my hot, hot eyelashes.

And when in the end my lifedays are over,
when in the end worms gobble my flesh:
Lord God, hear this prayer of mine –
let my dear ones live in Dreamland with me.

# P is for Parnok

Sophia Parnok was born in Taganrog in 1885. After years of travel and study, she settled and married in St Petersburg in 1907. Divorced in 1909, she became the lover of Marina Tsvetaeva, writing poetry that was declared 'against the law'. She retreated into translations and died in Moscow in 1933.

## To Khodaseyevitch

Memory of a child: these pears –
wrinkled, small, pinched,
and tucked with sour flesh
that sudden-pursed my mouth: just so
my pleasure in your poems'
harsh–bitter skelfs.

## Give Me Your Hand

Give me your hand, and come to our scarlet Heaven!…
Forget God's Enterprise Plan,
May has come back amidst Winter for us,
and the green wood has blossomed,

where our apple tree, bloomed above,
breezes us, swagged with sweet savour,
where the earth smells sweet as you are,
and butterflies ravish as they fly…

we are one year older, so what,
old wine that is one year more
still savours the game connoisseur…
My darling! Silver Eve! Be happy!

## Ghazals

Comfort of pain – your hand,
white bullbay flower – your hand.

One winter afternoon love tapped my door,
a sable-fur held in your hand.

Ah, butterfly on the stalk of my wrist,
it glimmered and stayed – not now – your hand!

And your hand fired what your enemies
damped – and I – but did not put out.

That megrim queen that fired
the fiery soft-sweetness in me – your hand!

It spurned me straight in the heart (how
could I complain, it is yours) – your hand.

## Grey Rose

Night. Clotted snow drops.
Moscow is asleep… but I…
ah, I am all awake
my love!

Ah, my blood starts to sing
in this stifling night…
Listen! Listen! Listen!
my love:

Silver rimes
in your petals.
O, grey rose,
my poems – for you!

You breathe beneath the white,
Rose of December,
and dole to me
your restless joy.

I drink and cry,
cry and drink,
and cry that I may lose you,
my Rose!


## In a White Night

It is not the sky – this stifled dome
atop the nude blank whiteness of the houses,
as if some careless thing
had spread a shroud on people and all things.

And dark – like light's shadow,
and light – like dark's reflection.
Was it day? Or was it night?
Or some disturbed half-dream?

I look upon all this with wiser eyes,
and thus my peace is gentler still,
I look upon your mouth, stopped
with kisses that are not mine.

So let it be, your lie-be-gentle, lie-unruffled
look beneath those lidded eyes –
surely, underneath this sky
anyone may be to blame!

# and for Pasolini

Pier Paolo Pasolini was born in Bologna in 1922. He wrote and made films, considering himself 'a petit-bourgeois shit who thinks he smells of perfume'. A life-long Communist, he believed that the working class could redeem the world. He was murdered on a beach in Ostia in 1975.


## Heading for Caracalla's Hotbaths

Heading for Caracalla's Hotbaths –
teen friends, astride
Rumis, Ducatis, man–modest,
man–cocky, coolly hiding
and showing the secret
of their hard–ons
in their warm trouser–rucks…
with curly hair and jumpers
the colour of now, they open
the night in an endless
carousel, penetrating night,
cool lords of the night…

Heading for Caracalla's Hotbaths –
a shepherd, stiff–chested, like
he was on his own Apennine hillslopes,
amongst tracks that smell of
age–old animals and holy ash
from berberlands – already spoiled,
under his dusty–rough beret,
hands in pockets – eleven when
he came here and now, still warm
with red sage, figs, olives,
a scruffy gagster with a roman smile…

Heading for Caracalla's Hotbaths –
an old family dad, workless,
who furious Frascati has washed out
to a goof-animal, happy,
with the old-iron chassis
of his smashed, bitsied body
rattling: his clothes-sack
holding a half-hunched back,
two scab-jammed thighs
and flapping pants under
his jacket pockets loaded
with stale paper bags. The face
laughs; the jaws grate, their
bones chawing words; he talks to himself,
stops, rolls some old fag-end,
a carcass where all youth
has stayed, flowering, like
a bonfire in a box or bowl:
they do not die who were not ever born.
Heading for Caracalla's Hotbaths…


## Going Too

I'm heading for Caracalla's Hotbaths too –
thinking – with my old, with my
breathtaking licence to think…
(to think there's still a god in me,
straying, drained, green,
but its voice human, human,
nearly a song). Oh to break out
of Misery Jail!
To be out of all this nervy fear that
makes the age-old nights so breathtaking!
There's something to share there with men who know disquiet,
and men who don't: men are ordinary wanters.
Top of the list, a pure white shirt!
Top of the list, good shoes,
lastable clothes! And a house in a place
where people don't hassle you,

a flat clear in the sun
with three, four rooms and a balcony,
a little alone, with roses and lemons…

Alone right to the bone, I have dreams too
that still hold me to the world
that I glimpse along, like I was just an eye…

I dream, my house, on Giancolo,
by Villa Pamphili, green all down to the sea:
a housetop brimmed with age-old sun,
always new-hard in Rome;
I'd make a sunroom on the balcony,
with dark curtains made of airy stuff:
and in one corner I'd put a table,
light, specially made, with a thousand
drawers, one for each written page,
so they don't cross the greedy
orders of my inspiration…
Ah, a bit of order, a bit of gentleness
in my work, in my life…
All round I'd put chairs, armchairs,
with a small antique table, and a few
pictures by cruel early Mannerists
in gold frames, to set against
the abstract forms in the sunroom…

And in the bedroom (a plain
small bed with flowered covers
sewn by Calabrian, Sardinian women)
I'd put up my collection
of still-loved pictures: beside
my Zigaina will be a beautiful Morandi,
a forties Mafai, a De Psis,
a small Rosai, a big Guttuso…

## Night's Triumph

A stack of orange ruins
blotted at night with the raw
colour of tartar, grassy bulwarks
of light pumice climbing
the sky: and, below, blanker,
Caracalla's Hotbaths, aahing
its still brownness of
grassless fields, trod brambles
at the burning moon. Everything drifts and thickens
through shafts of Caravaggio dust
and magnesium fans
cut in glittering smoke by the
little round of a country moon.
Out of that great sky descend
punters, heavy shadows, Puglian,
Lombardy grunts, Trastevere kids,
on their own, in gangs, that stop in the lowlaid
square, where the women, dried-up and brittle,
like jerked rags in the evening air,
redden and howl – like cheap
children, innocent grannies,
mothers: and in the heart of the close-round city
loaded with tram-rasp and light-tangles,
they rouse, in their own Caina,
the dust-stiff pants, who come in a
fitful abject gallop
over the garbage and the livid dew.


## Sex – Consolation for Unhappiness

Sex – consolation for unhappiness!
The whore rules, her throne
is a ruin, her land is a bit
of shat-on lawn, her sceptre
is a redleather handbag:
she barks at night, mucked and boiling,
like an old, old mother: defends

her stuff and her life.
Rushed round with pimps,
bellied and fagged,
Slav and Brindisi moustaches – her
pashas, princes: dark–
dealing their hundred lire works,
ssh-winks, swapping
watchwords: the left-out world, silent
round these self-leftouts,
still carcasses of things of prey.

But a new world sprouts from
the earth's rubbish: newborn laws
that are no-laws: newborn honour
that is dishonour…
newborn, howling power
and nobility in the heaps of hovels,
in the endless spaces where you think
the city ends; where, instead,
it starts again, bitter, starts again
a thousand times, bridges
and mazes, building sites and cuttings,
behind a storm-wave of skyscrapers
that cloud whole horizons.

In the easiness of love
the pained man feels himself just a man:
builds a belief in life, ends
hating those who live the other-life.
And sons sling themselves at all affairs,
safe in a world
that fears them, and their sex.
Their goodness in cruelty,
their strength in thoughtlessness,
their hope in having none.

## I Work All Day…

I work all day, monk-like,
and at night prowl, street-tom,
looking for love… I shall move
to the Church that I be made a saint.
I really do respond to spoof
mildly. I watch the lynch-staff
with a public eye.
I observe myself massacred with the cool
nerve of a scientist. I seem
to feel hate: instead, I write
poems full of proper love.
I study treachery as a fatal
phenomenon, like I was not its object.
I pity the young fascists
and the old; but I think they are forms
of the awfullest evil. I fight
with only the violence of reason.
Passive, like an all-seeing bird,
sky-beating, a conscience
that does not forgive.


## Prayer to My Mother

Hard to say with a son's words
what, at heart, I look like so little.

You are the one in the world that knows my heart,
what it always held, before all other love.

So I have to tell you what is awful to know:
my pain was born in your loving-kindness.

I can't replace you. So the life
you gave me is damned with loneliness.

I don't want to be alone. I have an endless
hunger for love, love of soulless bodies.

The soul is in you, is you, but you
are my mother, and your love is my slavery:

I lived childhood a slave of this high
immoveable feeling, of a great obligation.

It was the one way to feel life,
the one colour, the one form: now it's finished.


**But It Was Italy, Bare and Seething**

Rome, from the 50s till now, August 1966 –
I've done nothing but suffer and work wolfishly.
I taught – after a workless year and life's end –
in a private school for 27 dollars a month:
meanwhile my father
had come back to us:
we never talked about our escape – mine and my mother's.
An ordinary thing, a move in two loads.
We lived in a roofless, plasterless house,
a poorfolks' house, far on the city edge, near a prison.
A summer duststretch, a winter swamp –
but it was Italy, bare and seething,
with its boys, its women,
its jasmine scent, its poor-soup breath,
sunsets in the Aniene fields, rubbish-heaps,
and, with me, my unbroken dreams of poetry.
Poetry explained everything.
I thought that Italy, its portrait and its fate,
turned on what I wrote about it,
in those poems soaked with now's reality,
not nostalgic now, like I'd earned it with my sweat –
so what if, some days,
I didn't even have a hundred lire to get a shave,
my sparing figure, though fitful and mad,
was in that moment, in many ways,
like the people I lived with:
so we were real brothers, equals at least –
so, I believed, I could understand them, truly –

## Rome, Evening

Down the streets of Rome go trolleybuses,
trams full of men heading home: but
you're going out somewhere, in a hurry,
obsessed, like some long-suffered work
waits for you, when the rest go home.
Dinner is nearly done, and the breeze
smells of sullen family warmth
leaked through a thousand kitchens and
the long, lit streets
where shinier stars look down.
In the smarter streets there's peace,
shut-up, smug and
vile: what they all want,
to fill every evening of their lives.
Ah, you don't want that: to be
innocent in a guilty world…
So you're going down, down the bent,
dark road that goes to Trastevere:
and here, unmoving, disturbed, like something
unburied from the mud of different lives –
some place for men who still can grab one more
day back from death and sadness –
all Rome is at our feet…

I get off, cross the Garibaldi Bridge
close to the wall, my knuckles
against the gnawed stone rim,
hard in the careful warmth
that night breathes on the vaults
of warm plane trees. Leaden, flat attics
and their sallow blocks cram
the washed-out sky on the far bank:
a dull tread of concrete slabs.
And I see, walking down the
crackbone pavement – no, smell –
the great family land,
wild, dull, stamped with
aged stars and dinning windows:

dim and humid, summer gilds it
with a foul stink, the wind,
splashing down from Lazio fields,
pours over busrails and housefronts.

And down here the embankment stinks
with a crowded heat so
closeabout it is its own place:
Sublicio Bridge as far as Gianicolo –
the stench laces the drunkenness
of the life that isn't life.
The unclean signs – old trampdrunks,
ancient whores, packs of nobody's
boys that have come and gone:
unclean human clues,
man–infected, that expose them,
violent and quiet, their low, innocent
pleasures, their haveless ends.


## Bellsong

When evening ebbs in these fountains
my home is a run colour.

I am gone, I remember the frogs,
the moon, the sad whirr of crickets.

Vespers ring and waste on the fields:
I am dead to the bellsong.

Don't worry, stranger: my sweet flight arches
over the empty land. I am a ghost of love

who comes back to his home that was gone.

## My Deathday

In some city, Trieste or Udine,
    along some limetreed street,
in spring, while the leaves
    are shifting colour,
    I'll fall down dead
under a throbbing sun,
    blond, tall,
and shut my eyes,
and leave the shining sky alone.

Under a hot–green limetree
    I'll fall down in death's
dark, ungathering
    the limes and the sun.
    And beautiful boys
will run in the light
    I've lately lost
haring from school
all tousled.

# Q is for Queen Mary

Mary Stuart was born in 1542 in Linlithgow Palace. Amidst official letters and documents, poetry always had its place, recording and expressing her political and personal ups and downs. She was executed in 1587 at Fotheringhay.


**(Ode on the death of her husband, King Francis II, when he was sixteen, and she seventeen)**

My song is measured-sad –
a grave and sound complaint –
to cast a keening eye
on more than any loss –
and in my stung sighs
spend my best years.

Is such ill fate –
such hurt sadness –
amongst the cruel
befallen ends
of Dame Fortune –
that you – my heart, my eye –
look upon the bier and coffin.

In my sweet springtime –
flower of my young days –
to pain at every sense
upon the ends of grief –
and have no pleasure in no thing
but longing long and loss.

He who was my delight
is now my harshest hurt –
the bright and brightest day
is black and hiding night –

and nothing is so wonderful
that I wish it mine.

In heart and eye I have
a painted thing of him
that shows my grieving loss –
and my pale face
of fainted violets –
that is fainted love.

For this strange hurt
I cannot stay still –
but change and change about –
so I rush out of my sadness –
for my worse and my better
are both most empty places.

Wherever I am –
woods or fields –
in day's dawning
or the evening time –
endlessly my heart lives
the loss of one who is gone.

And sometimes somewhere
I see, I sense
the sweet sight of his eyes
in a cloud –
then suddenly I see tombs
in the rain.

If I am at rest –
sleepy on my couch –
I hear his words to me –
I feel him touch me –
at work – at Court-time –
always near me.

I can see nothing else
for his glory in the way –
and my heart will not say yes
to anything I reach for –
disallowed perfection
in this trial.

Put an end to this song –
this sad complaint –
whose burden shall be –
for the torn apart
of true love and not empty
there will be no less of loss.

### (8th sonnet to Lord Bothwell)

While you made love, she played the maid –
if you suffered love's sweet heat –
that comes from love's great over-feeling –
her touch displayed her dreary heart –
taking no pleasure from your great warmth.
Her clothes – truly – made plain
she had no fear that wanting style
might score her from your loyal heart.
I saw in her no fear of death for you
due to her husband and her lord.
All in all, you are all her good –
yet she never prized nor valued
that greatest pleasure – for it was not hers –
though now she says she loved it most.

## (Sonnet to Queen Elizabeth)

An only thought – that safes me and alarms –
bitter and sweet – changes endless in my heart –
clouds on me between doubt and hope
while peace and calm fly from me.
So – sister dear – if this letter draws on
the fond desire to see you that makes me forward thus –
it is because I am condemned to pain and sadness
if some answer does not quickly come.
I have seen a ship drop anchor
upon the high tide – near to port –
and the bright sky cloud.
Thus I am in worry and in fear –
not from you but from unsteady times
when Fortune breaks – its double – sail and rigging.


## (Sonnet written at Fotheringhay Castle)

Ah what am I? – and what use my life? –
I am no more than a body stripped of its heart –
a nothing-shadow – a thing of misery –
with nothing now more than a death in life.
O enemies – envy me no more –
who has no more desire alive for greatness.
I have done with too much sadness –
and cannot see your anger quickly tempered.
And you – my friends – still truly dear –
remember that – heartless and lifeless –
I cannot do good things –
I hope only for the end of calamity
and that – punished here so much –
I will have my part of eternity's happiness.

# and for Quasimodo

Salvatore Quasimodo was born in Modica, Sicily, in 1901. He was an engineer until the age of 37, after which he dedicated himself to writing poetry and translating classic texts. He won the Nobel Prize in 1959, and died in Naples in 1968.

## Thanatos Athanatos

Do I have to eat my words then, Tumour-
God, Liveflower-God,
and start out now with a no to the shady
'I am' stone, and say yes yes to death
and write on every grave the one
thing bound to us – 'thanatos athanatos'?
Without a name to not forget the dreams,
tears, rage of this man
undone by unfinished Musts?
Our question-answer changes: now it
turns maybe absurd. There
past the fog and smoke, inside the trees,
the power-drive of leafshoots looks out,
the river that pushes its banks is real.
Life is not a dream. Man is real,
and his green-eyed lament of silence.
God of silence, open solitude.

## A Street in Agrigentum

There is still a wind I remember struck
in manes of horses pitched-
pelting over plains, wind
that blots and gnaws the sandstone and the heart
of moping man-pillars, keeled
on the grass. Old soul, galled

and grey, come back into that wind, sniff
the frail moss that coats
these giants pushed down by heaven.
How all alone in your staying place!
And more mournful-hurt to hear the sound
that moves off to the sea again
where Hesperus steals in the first of morning
the jewharp sadly buzzes
in the throat of the cartman climbing
the moon-sharpened hill
among the mutter of Moorish olive trees.


## Nearly a Madrigal

Sunflower leans west
and day quick now drops in its
wrecked eye and summer's air
clots already kinks leaves and the
building site haze. The last sky-game
moves off with a dry clouds' slide
and lightning jangle. Again,
and years since, darling, we are held
by the change-trees tight in a circle
of canal boats. But the day is still ours
and it's still that sun that takes itself away
with the thread of its sweet beams.

I have no memories anymore, don't want to remember;
memory comes from death,
life has no end. Every day
is ours. One will shut forever,
and you with me, when it seems late.
Here on the canal bank, seesawing
feet like children,
we watch the water, the first branches in
its dimming greenness.
And the man that comes quietly near
does not hide a knife in his hand,
but a geranium flower.

## Rain and Iron Colours

You said: death, silence, aloneness,
like love, life. Words
of our brittle pictures.
And the wind came light every morning
and time the colour of rain and iron
went by on stones,
on our wrapped damned drone.
Still truth is far away.
And tell me, cross-cleft man,
and you with heavy bloody hands,
how do I answer the askers?
Now, now: before other silence
enters eyes, before other wind
rises and other rust blossoms.


## Epitaph for Bice Donetti

With her eyes on rain and on night-elfs,
she's there, in Area Fifteen in Musocco,
the Emilian woman I loved
in young life's sad time.
A little while ago Death enjoyed her
while she quietly looked at the autumn wind
shivering plane tree branches and leaves
in an ashy suburb house.
Her face still bright with surprise,
like it surely was in childhood, electric-struck
by the fire-eater high on the cart.
O passers-by, pushed on by other dead ones,
stop at grave eleven sixty
for a minute to say hello
to one who never mourned the man
still left here, hated, with his poems,
one like many, labouring in dreams.

## Lament for the South

Red moon, wind, your North-woman
colour, sprawl of snow…
by now my heart is in these grasslands,
in these fog-hooded waters.
I have left behind the sea, the harsh-sound
seashell blown by Sicily shepherds,
the singsong of carts along the road
where the carob shivers in stubble haze,
I have left behind the heron-pass and crane-flight
in the green upland air
for the land and rivers of Lombardy.
But man will shout the fate of a homeland wherever he is.
No one will take me South again.

Oh, the South is tired of dragging the dead
on the shores of malaria swamps,
and tired of loneliness, tired of chains,
and tired of all the curses
in its mouth of all the breeds who have
bawled death with the echo of its well-holes,
who have lapped its heart-blood.
So its boys go back to the mountains,
hustle their horses under blankets of stars,
eat new-red acacia flowers
along the trail, still red, still red.
No one will take me South again.

And this winter-loaded evening
is still ours, and here I repeat for you
my counterpoint nonsense
of sweetness and rage,
a lament of love without love.

# R is for Renaud

Suzanne Renaud was born in Lyon in 1889. 'The Catholic poet of difficult times', she divided her married life between France and Czechoslovakia, and translated much literature between the two countries' languages. She died in Havlíčkův Brod in 1964.


## Between Dogday and Nightwolf

Between dogday and nightwolf
the book shuts,
and the less sure hand
drops sudden
the needle
and the gleaming thimble
to the sewsheet
between dogday and nightwolf;
between dogday and nightwolf
the doubting,
hutch-skimming day
flies like a filcher.


## Winter End

At the edge of the puddled pond
the village is white
like a basket of eggs;

no flower disclosed
in the raw orchard
upon pink eiderdown
blue eiderdown.

But there, beneath the branches
of the crabbed apple tree
two wee goats that dance
so whitely white
one pities them;

winter end.

## August Moon

Tonight I saw the alien moon
angel–grand,
red as the once–was sea
put its darkling barns ajar
the Field of Blood from Heaven's depths
where Hell-harvests burn.

## Nightbirds

Two calls
out from the garden's dark
fall at the lucent night.
Two calls? No,
two singing tears.

A shook call: 'Father, where are you?
Father, where are you?'
Moon and silence.

This far call, this lost one's call
turns the hinges of silence,
half opens the door to the secret
swiftly lost;
'Father, where are you?'

The tree head–heavy with Knowing
shivers, sighs and hushes.
Moon and silence.

## Rope-Coloured Land

Rope-coloured land
where the wind sings
under a waiting cloud-winged sky
its long orphan keen.
Land of bare trudge-pilgrim paths
where apple trees bend on their backs,
trailing aloneness and age
on their fardels of sorrow and winds;
land of hard trees with fruits of longsuffering
where the evening forest lifts a dazzled front,
Veronica wipes the face of silence
where, tatter on tatter,
great loves unreturned
burn out in the dark.


## Morning Light

The ill-meaning night, the mad spider
that drags the thread Dismay
out of the heart
leaves to hide itself in the fireplace.
Then at the garden brink who has thrown
upon a bush this enchanted veil?
Who has weaved our night of frights
into a lattice then so clear, trembled and gold,
that all September wept upon
its tender trap for tears.


## Nightpiece I

Night, rain, a breath of wind…
O my true memory, what have you shook
down in your sift?
A little wheat and so much chaff.
Night, rain, a breath of wind…
sad heart, who dreams about

like some clamant tramp,
how often, shrunk beneath the catslide,
have you found the inn empty!
Night, rain, a breath of wind…


**Nightpiece II**

Wind breathes, in the years' deeps
harsh wind with dead branches
the past clacks like a door
unopened still and still unclosed.
O much loved ones, too little loved,
regret pipes under the door
the tears of your closed eyes
toll in our disarmed hearts
as in a hollow of dead leaf.
The past clacks like a door
unopened still and still unclosed.
The hour wakes and says, 'What matter?'


**The Nuts**

This time of year
in my country the nuts fall,
fall to the feet of old crosses,
fall to the blenched grass;
and when the wind stirs up a keening bark
into their unwritten fall,
how the soul groaned to be born!
The passer-by may crush them,
like a dry crack of laughter,
a sob that dies all dumb
in the cold way's gutter.

# and for Radauskas

Henrikas (Henri) Radauskas was a Lithuanian born in Krakow in 1910. 'A poet who made a personal universe of the things of the world, where they could be gently managed', he worked for ten years as a chair machinist in the USA, where he died in 1970.

## Angel of Death

Comes over the greystone yard,
blackwing, slatefeather gleam.
Strokes tree, water and cat,
glances at the day's mirror.

Puddle shivers, though wind has died,
cat on the doorstep attacks air
like a mouse. Tree's blood starts to clot,
day sets blotched on rust grass.

Oak door, a hundred old, yawls
like a baby. Invalid's eyes see
through yellow fog: rainbows
pour into earth, parrot-shrieking.

Clock meters out time for the living,
spider hangs his net between stars,
and angel, at the fireplace,
turns into smoke, ember, ash.

## Sunday

Twenty-year-dead room:
old woman's shadow yawns, winds an empty
coffee grinder, clock says Sunday,
cuckoo hushed still, guest stabbed in the pub.

Sleeping woman reads a burned book:
*Horrible Story of the Devil Belphegor.*
Saturn's scrappy lines on her palms.
Two-thick walls filled with ducats, bones.

Washed-out voice clips up the cellar stairs,
candle-dribbling, tear-dribbling coloratura.
Wall slits, rubber girl droops,
violins bear the blood-heart into the garden.

Giant hooting maple tree knocks on a red
coffin prettied with flutes and fiorituras.
'Poveri fiori'. Venomed violets faint.
Voice's shadow pours into the missing house.


**Midday**

Yelling he didn't have a soul
he bomped to earth from the crooked tower.
Under him lakes money-glittered
and grass lapped milk bubbles.

Flying shadow yelled pleased.
Grey air didn't hear it.
King's dog chipper chased an elk,
scarlet orchards apple-choked.

Italian no-legs angel crept along
pulling a big bag of tin birds
for orphans. Sweet sedge shadows
said to cockle-shell Beauty on the bank:
'Why do you hide lips and eyes?'

## Muse

Dressmaking muse out of Denis's picture
puts sewing down on the seat, gets up,
walks down a summer-blank road
all Chinese-sallow face.
Check dress starts up the stairs
and under her step an oaken voice
meters word-runs into iambs.

Goes like the wind through the
heavy slept door and quickly
swells like a statue there in the room.
Children see the blank stone face
squeal and run, they try,
she heaves them out the window,
geranium, canary,
children, wing-waving,
land like angels in the Square.
Flower warbles birdlike in the road,
canary blooms
light-yellow blossom. Stone
gives the man pen and paper book
and starts to dictate, sluggish.


## Mechanical Angel

Mechanical Angel's job is not that hard:
look after lightning, serve bread and wine,
watch through windows how fire scales walls,
chat to streetlights about the old days.

Mechanical Angel's job is not that hard:
feed tower-Chimeras once every hundred years,
walk lightly so metal does not DONG,
dress cold caryatids with fog.

Mechanical Angel's job is not that hard:
stop up the door, don't let Death in,
if she gets in then show her some brother asleep
and persuade her he has no soul.

# S is for Södergran

Edith Södergran was born in 1892 in St Petersburg. Her family was Finnish-Swedish, and she wrote in Swedish. Diagnosed with TB at seventeen, she passed years in sanatoria, while her published 'modernist' poetry was greeted with hostility, indifference or incomprehension. She died at home in Raviola in 1923.

## Three Sisters

One sister loved strawberries sweet and wild,
the second loved red roses,
the third loved garlands for the dead.

Sister One married:
I have heard she is happy.

The Second Sister loved with a heart complete:
I heard she turned out sad.

Sister Three became a Saint:
I heard that Life's deathless crown will be hers.

## Wish

Out of all our sunshine world
I wish for just a garden bench,
a warmsleep cat…
to sit there
with a letter near my heart,
just one short letter.
That is the picture of my dream.

**I Saw a Tree...**

I saw a tree, greater than the rest,
and hung all round with cones I could not reach;
I saw a mighty church, its doors all wide,
and all who came out there were pale and strong
and ready for death;
I saw a smiling, painted woman
throwing dice to try what hap she had
and saw her lose.

There was a circle drawn about these things,
a circle no one oversteps.


**Walking, I Took My Way about the Solarsystems**

Walking,
I took my way about the solarsystems,
until, until I found the first thread of my red gown.
I know myself by now.
In space somewhere my heart hangs,
streaming sparks, thuddering in air,
holding out to other worldless hearts.


**The Land That Is Not**

I long for the land that is not,
because I am too tired to want all there is.
The moon, with silver runes, brings word to me
of the land that is not.
A land where all our dreams are strangely given,
a land where our fetters all fall,
a land where we calm our bloody heads in moon-mist.
My life was hot folly.
But one thing I found, one thing I have won –
is the way to the land that is not.
In the land that is not
my darling walks with a glittered crown.

Who is my darling? Dark is the night,
and the stars shake in their answer.
Who is my darling? What is his name?
Heaven arches higher and higher
and the earth-child is drunken in far endless fogs
and knows no answer.
But the earth-child is sure, and only sure.
And reaches his arms on on higher than Heaven.
And answer comes: I am who you love, and always will.

## and for Salinas

Pedro Salinas was born in Madrid in 1891. 'Eminent, learned and difficult', he taught at universities including the Sorbonne, Cambridge, Johns Hopkins and Seville. Part of the 'Generation of '27' group, which included Lorca and Guillén, he died in Boston in 1951.

### To the One I Love

To her, the one I love,
not to the one that comes surrendering,
that comes falling
with wornness, millstoned,
like water by rain-law,
all down, sure catch
of the listless ground grave.
To this her, the one I love,
to the one that comes conquering
with striding from freedom,
with want and push
and love-want, charge,
waterspout, heron-soar,
shot – arrowshot –
over her victoried cares,
all up, winning the sky.

### What Birds?

Bird? Birds?
One bird in the whole world, one,
maybe, that flies with a thousand wings, and sings
with a thicket of chitter, all, all alone?
And earth and sky mirrors? And air
air-glass, and the great bird
spawns its loneness

alone in a thousand appearings?
(Is this
why we call them birds?)
Or maybe there is no bird?
Is that them then,
mustbe vasty plural, like the sea,
boundless-gathered, wing-swell,
where looking looks for and the soul desires
to tell the truth of one lone bird
from its endless end, that wonderful one?


## Nightwater, Stalling Snake...

Nightwater, stalling snake,
small whistle and unwary way:
which day snow, which day sea? Tell me tell me.
Which day cloud, echoback
of you and a dry dead riverbed?
Tell me tell me.
– Not telling: you have me in your lips,
I will give you kisses but not clarities.
And let night-pities be enough
and leave the rest to darkness,
for I was made
for thirsts of lips that never ask.


## Master of Matter

Close darked in,
the world was black: blank.
When a terse tug
– line-shaped, curve-shaped –
outdrew the flame.
Crystal, oak, lit up –
the joy in them,
in light, in lines, to be
a gleam and living strake!
When the flame is out,

uncatchable reality,
this shape, that shade,
they slip away.
And live there, or in doubt?
Nostalgia noses up, slow,
not from the moon, not love,
not infinity. Nostalgia
of a vase on a table.
There then?
I look for where they were.
The Sweeper of Shadows
tries the hand. Dim-
shifting tracks, anxiety behind.
Swift as flame
the highest joy rises
from blackness: touch-light.
Come in the world of sureness.
Touches the crystal, cool, hard,
touches the wood, rough.
There then!
The hushed and perfect life,
no colour, settles itself to me,
certain, lightless, felt:
deep reality, mass.

# T is for Tiburge

Tiburge (de Sarenom) was born about 1130, in Provence. A *trobairitz* (female troubadour), this fragment of a Canso is her only surviving poetry. She was 'beautiful and intelligent, beloved of all men and respected by all women' and 'wrote good poems'. She died around 1198.

## Fragment of a Canso

Sweet bonny boy, the truth is easy writ:
that since the hour you honoured to admit
my own unto your love, no hour expires
without my heart's delight, my strait desires;
and still none passes without want for you,
to see you, sweetheart, new and new and new;
nor have I ever doubted, or walked free
until you, vexed and gone, came back to me;
nor...

## and for Tyutchev

Fyodor Ivanovich Tyutchev was born in Ovstug in 1803. He believed himself a mere 'poet of bagatelles', but, as a vigorous Slavophile, had variously unpleasant things to say about the Vatican, the Ottoman Empire, and Poland. Though he spoke French better, he wrote in Russian. He died in 1873 in St Petersburg.

### Summer Evening

The worldhead has wheeled away the hot sun's round,
and the sea wave sponged twilight's soft burning.

Now the bright stars rise, hung high,
and lift their heavens-dome with dewy tops.

The wide air-river pours from sky to earth,
whose heart breathes easier and free,
lightened from such heat.

And a sweet, sweet shudder starts through nature's veins,
as if her fervid feet have touched spring water.

### You Saw Him...

You saw him then, in the Smart Set –
now faddy smiling,
now gloomy, gross, morose and all dark-minded –
the poet – and you snubbed him.

See the moon: all day, like a drawn cloud,
it swoons in the sky –
but night comes – and the lambent god
shines on the sleeping woods.

## Predestination

Love, love – so custom says –
is a joining of soul to suited soul –
their meeting, their mixing,
their unchosen cross…
and… their unchosen fight…

And for which is the tenderer
in the battle of two unequal hearts,
ah, certain and sure,
Love – hurting, sadly feeling-dying –
wears out at last…


## Leaves

Pine and spruce
can poke up all winter,
ragged in storm and snow, they sleep.
Their scrubby green,
like hedgehog prickles,
does not yellow,
but is never bright.

We, the unheavy brood,
flower up and flibble
just a while,
twig-guests.
All the sunny summer through
we are beauty-full,
alive with sun,
dew-ducking!

but now the birds don't sing,
flowers don't flower,
sunshine fails,
breezes fall.
Why do we hang on,
senselessly sere?

Why don't we loose,
and go too?

O turbulent wind,
heave harder, harder!
Rip us now, now off these
stale branches!
Rip us and wrest us away,
now, now – to fly,
fly with you!


**Insomnia**

Time's boring war,
the dragged story of night.
Its language strange and lone,
but known, like conscience.

Who can hear with no heartache,
amidst the universal hush,
the muffling groan of time,
the long, foreboding voice of goodbye.

We feel the earth an orphan,
caught by a fightless fate.
And we, at odds and arms with nature,
are left to find our selves.

And our life, there, there,
like a ghost on the edge of the earth,
pales our days and friends
into a greying farness.

And a new young brood
has flowered under the sun
and borne us and our age, my friends,
long gone towards nothing.

Now and then a sad procession
walks the midnight hour;
now and then a metal voice,
our deadmarch, mourns us.

# U is for Ullmann

Regina Ullmann was born in St Gallen in 1884. She moved to Munich in 1902, and began to write poems, poetic prose and stories, many of a Catholic bent. She died in Bavaria in 1961.


## Waking

I lay on, limbless, in you,
the dark's deep rock:
cold as stone, and comfort-lost.

Then felt, aquick, how day
ravelled itself in the life of light,
flamewise, warm as love,
and fastened in the smallest things.

Then I was awake.
But still I heard a silver sound,
someone's clash upon a cymbal,
and my angel's morning walk.


## The Graveyard Burns...

The graveyard burns,
lit by bright wind,
dragging the old crosses down
into itself,
turning flower-blossom to crystal gauze,
dancing to its windorgan's
blowy songs,
and winding round, and winding up
into lilac-clumps and rosebushes,
and lighting old lindens with sweet smells,

like candles about death's box,
which is no more.
For it is all full of life,
and the sparklings fall drop-drop upon the field,
which mows its ripened self...


## The Loner

Strange man,
you passed me,
and now I see you standing
out there, far off.
I go in.
I know, I know
that I'm all right.
The oil
in my jug
has not dried out.
And if I get hungry
I shall take myself by the hand.
And pity for you
does not help me.
Ah, of course, it's hard.
You would freeze in my dress,
and be thirsty.
But I am solitude
and love myself
like all that is.


## Storm in a Poppyfield

Once I walked in a poppyfield in a storm,
years ago —
and it was my dress
red silk and wide as wide...
like silkwisp poppies upside-down.
And a wheel of it whacked off me and lapped the field
from harm, all harm —

and I was called to witness a higher world,
that bade me to that red field
that day, so many years ago!

## and for Uhland

Johann Ludwig Uhland was born in Tübingen in 1787. 'Manly and straightforward', he wrote poems, eight volumes on the German language, and studies of folk legends, medieval manuscripts, sagas and troubadours. He was also a professor, an attorney and a politician. He died in Tübingen in 1862.

### Once I Had a Comrade

Once I had a comrade,
you couldn't find one better,
the drum drummed up for battle,
he marched in step beside me,
step by step in step,
step by step in step.

A bullet came flying,
meant for me or you?
It took him clean away,
he's lying at my feet,
just like a piece of me,
just like a piece of me.

He's holding out his hand,
while I reload my gun,
'I can't give you my hand,
stay in eternal life,
my good comrade,
my good comrade.'

## The Black Knight

Whitsun, the Happy Festival.
Woods and wolds rejoice.
The king said:
'A fat Spring shall break
out of all the walls
of the old Courtcastle too!'

Drums and trumpets blared,
red banners flapped merrily.
The king watched from his balcony:
and the jousting knights
all fell before
the king's strong son.

But a Black Knight rode up
last to the lists.
'Sir! What is your name and blazon?'
'If I told you,
you would tremble and funk:
I am a great-realmed prince.'

When he rode to the tilt
Heaven's dome went dark,
and the castle started to shake.
At the first blow
the son fell off his horse
and could hardly get up.

Pipes and fiddles called for dancing,
torches twinkled in the halls;
a huge shadow pitched in
and mannerly asked
for the king's daughter
and started to dance with her.

He danced in a black-iron gown,
danced eerily,
cold-noosed about her body.
The bright flowers fell
from her breast and hair,
withered to the ground.

All the knights and ladies
came to the great table.
The old king sat down,
worried at heart,
between his son and daughter
and looked at them, silently thinking.

Both the children looked pale.
The visitor raised his cup:
'Gold wine will make you better.'
The children drank,
thanked him kindly:
'This drink is chilly.'

Son and daughter hugged
their father: their cheeks
bleached completely.
Wherever the grey-shocked
father looked he saw
his children dying.

'Ah, You have taken both
beautiful children in their young joy.
I am joyless: take me too!'
Then the terrible visitor spoke
with a hollow, thudding voice:
'Old man! I crush Spring roses!'

## Hush of Spring

Oh, don't dig me down deep in the dark ground
under the green green world!
When I am put away,
lie me down in the long deep grass.

And I will lie happy in grass and flowers
while a far-off flute tootles
and way, way above me
shiny spring clouds go their ways.


## A Trip Home

Don't bust now, footbrig – ricketyshake now,
don't slip now, bluffrocks – heavy-justabout to,
don't end yet world, don't fall yet sky,
till I am with my sweet love.

# V is for Vivien

Renée Vivien was born (Pauline Tarn) in London in 1877. Disappointed by affairs with an American heiress, a Rothschild baroness, and the wife of a Turkish diplomat, she decamped to Egypt, Japan, Hawaii, the Middle East and America. She died in 1909 from a combination of anorexia, drugs and alcohol.

## Age Approaches

I cannot pretend I am wrong anymore.
I am here, and bound to be, face to face
with the inevitable, and the terror:
I confront the too-true mirror, and my soul weeps.

Every useless physic stokes my heart,
for none returns my plundered youth...
I have borne too-all the killing weight of life
and greet today my last despair.

Yesterday, the struggled, awful effort seemed so careless-light.
Today, shock shuts down my voice.
I feel my sometime soul die inside,
the shadowed horror of my rotting ebb.

## Evening Roses

Seaborne roses, sunset roses,
and you that come from far with rose-charged hands!
I breathe your beauty. The falling sun turns rain
into its golden cinders and its rose-tinc't dust.

Seaborne roses, sunset roses.

A coloured thought holds my eyelids down.
I wait, half-knowing what I wait for with no hope,
before the shield-brass sea,
and you are coming now, to bring me roses…

O heaven and sunset roses! O my roses!


## Your Royal Youth Has the Sadness…

Your royal youth has the sadness
of the North, where fog wipes colour out,
you cross with tears faction and desire,
Hamlet-grave, and pale as Ophelia.

You pass, as she, in flarings of fair madness,
lavishing songs and flowers,
as he, beneath hurt-hiding pride,
your still set stare, and its forgetting.

Smile, fair love, or dream, dark lover,
your twofold self attracts, a double-magnet,
and your flesh burns with the cold passion of a spill.

My unquiet heart is troubled when I see
your rapt and Prince's face, your pure blue eyes,
now This, now That, and both in one.


## Coming to Mytilene

Out of my deep past, I come back to you,
Mytilene, upon the play of centuries,
and bring my fire, my youth, my faith,
my love, like fairing spices,
Mytilene, along the play of centuries,
out of my deep past, I come back to you.

I find your waves, your olive trees, fruit vines,
and blue blue sky, wherein I melt and sink away,
your ships, your mountains and their high design,
your frantic, fevered cricket-cries,
beneath your blue sky, wherein I melt and sink away,
I find your waves, your olive trees, your fruit vines.

Take into your orchard fields two women,
canorous, love-careful island,
in Asiatic, thick and jasmine balm,
unforgetful still of Sappho and her flames,
canorous, love-careful island,
take into your orchard fields two women.

Lesbos, golden fieldflanks, give us your ancient soul,
retune the lyres and voices
and the old dear laughter and the yester-songs,
which touched the kisses of all ages gone,
you who hold within the lyre and the sweet-voiced echoes,
Lesbos, golden fieldflanks, give us your ancient soul.

Call back the white shifts' evening dance,
the fair and nutbrown lights of shocks of hair,
the golden chalice, chain and mirror,
the hyacinth and the soft sweet whispered sigh,
call back the brightness of the heavened hair,
and the white shifts that pass upon the evening hour.

And when the lovers, laid upon your beds of crackled weed,
passed drowsy words among, and half-said lines,
you mixed your rose and peachy scents
with all the drawn, soft whispers after kisses,
and now we lie, passing drowsy words among, and half-said lines,
upon your beds of crackled weed.

Mytilene, brilliant and glory of the sea,
unquiet and eternal as she was,
be today the altar of yesterday's temulent heart,
for Sappho slept with the Immortal,
and so receive us kindly, for love of her,
Mytilene, brilliant and glory of the sea!

# and for Verhaeren

Emile Verhaeren was born in Sint-Amands in 1855. 'A tornado of
indomitable personality, who cared not at all for bourgeois rules', he
wrote an immense body of work, concerned with rural decline and the
fate of the poor. He fell under a train at Rouen Station in 1916.


## Bread Cooking

The helps made Sunday bread,
best milk, best wheat,
bent brows, jutty elbows out of sleeves,
sweat in them, and dropping in the doughtub.

Their hands, fingers, all of them, meant business,
their bodies budged in great bodices,
their thumping two-fists dobbed in dough,
punched bunshapes like breast flesh.

The black wood cracked in kindled strakes,
and off the cook-board's edge, on trays in twos,
they shoved the pale soft dough into the oven's belly.

And the flames, through their way-in mouths,
like a huge hot gaggle of scarlet dogs,
jumped and barked to bite their faces.


## The Stable

This cattle mob, magnificent, stuffed
the offside stable, by the two-storey dungheaps,
its shutters shut, in a hot sleep,
under the pack of crabbit sunshine.

In the damp heat of the rested farm,
in the steam-up of stale cow hay,
the bulls reared their swelling boulder-rumps,
the cows mooed softly, eyes half shut.

Midday rang, the stable-gang swept the stalls,
filled them with hay, lavender, sage,
that the cattle fretted with heavy chaw.

And the numb tough fingers of the milkers
pulled down upon the hanging udders
and clenched the dangling teats wantingly.


## Ice

This evening, a huge blank sky, all strange, all air,
cold with stars, all shut
to men's prayers – a huge blank sky came:
a seen Forever stopped in its mirror.

Ice ringed this gold-and-silver endlessness,
ice ringed its winds, its shorelines, its silence,
its plains, its seas; ice that bit
the far-off blue, where starlight shot its spears.

All unchanging still. The feel of iron, a vice
screws up your heart, gloomy white,
and fright grabs this winter, on and on,
and a God-surprise in glacier glory.


## Milk

In a low, narrow cellar, near
a window of north-sent light, the cruses
cooled the white pooled milk
in their fat, red, earthen roundness.

Perhaps say, sleeping in their dark corner,
they looked like waterlilies, huge-opening in waves of slowness,
their helpings kept beneath white lids,
held fair for angel eating only in the dark.

Two sat lines of fat pots.
And great plates of hams and gammons,
skin-popping, wax-shade meat puddings
and buffy tarts all sugar-strung,
great galumphs of guts and flesh –
but there, across, the milk stayed immaculate and cold.

## The Trained Trees

The mighty trained trees held out their long branches,
where fruit belit its flesh and throng,
like seeing red balloons in greenness
burning in the buzzing funfair nights.

For twenty years, through winter hail,
evening freeze and morning frost,
they clung themselves on brickgaps, blockcracks,
climbing roofwards, up and up.

And now they mass the walls with showy splash,
and on the high pale gables, pears and apples
plump, all proud, their ripe and purpled breasts.

The giant trunks, crazy-split, sweat gum;
the roots mine to the nearest creeks,
and the leaves gleam like bird-flap.

## Harvests

Right with the morning sunshine up –
enamel glint on a huge sapphire –
and the birds' air-detail lovesongs,
the whole farm burst to work.

Hither, thither, jumble-quick, rowdy shouts –
and crazy chooks ascrabble,
scooting, capering, flapping, scramble again,
spiked their screechy tizz with it all.

And with the sun folks went out together down the hedgerows
to grub the willow-warded fields,
cut and pile and bring the haycarts in.

Above, the chaffies, siskins, orioles sang,
the fields scented the sky; and farmhelps
dotted the green squares with red smocks.


## The Mill

The mill turns in its evening set, so slow
on a sad and heavy sky,
turns, turns, and its dreggy sail
is drear, scant, dull and tired, without end.

Since sunrise its sticks, like pleading arms,
have reached and dropped: and now, look,
drop again, down in the blackish air,
in the utter quiet of dead nature.

A sick winter day sleeps on the villages,
clouds tired of their dark travels,
and along their shadow-shading hedgerows
trackruts roll at a dead horizon.

Round a stale pond, some birch huts
sit pinched and poor.
Brass lamps blink their ceilings,
and worm light into their window-nooks.

And on the great plain, by the dull water,
these numb houses watch, below the low sky,
with worn and slack-eyed panes,
the old mill turning, tired, turning, dying.

## Kitchen

At the back, the trammel, its hook hanged,
the fireplace agleam like a red puddle,
flames biting, biting, biting the fireback,
fretting the rude-scened iron.

The fire kicked at its hood beetled
over it like a fair-stall tent-top,
where shiny knickknacks, wood, pewter, lacquer,
glittered in little by the bent brazier.

Lightstreaks shot like emerald squirts
here, there, all about, jabbing
brightness into glassware and enamel dishes.

Watching some spark fire and fall there,
it seems like – the fire so crumbled to bits –
the sun sieved through a windowpane.


## Village

Roughcast walls, tat roofs,
bridge, towpath,
the mill making its cross
over the village, top to bottom.

Lean-tos, houses,
like dead flotsam things,
a sleeping fishnet; and dry fish
hung by the door.

A dog starts, barks, barks;
shouts go past, heavy, sepulchral;
the carpenter cuts his wood;
something gropes in the shadow.

Jobs make their muddled jangles,
and tire, one by one.
Behind a wall more murmurs,
the last paternoster's patter.

A woman with lank hands
gropes with her stick-end,
door to door, along paths
all evening-made. It is autumn.

Next comes bony winter.
Thin, shrifty winter,
when people are luckless
more than souls in Purgatory.


## The Big Room

And here, what was the Guestroom,
where a stranger got board and goodwill,
where sons were born, where forefathers died,
and bodies were bundled huge in their biers.

Fundays, fairdays and festival,
the farm played its holiday here,
and the Farmer, dead and gone now,
on her throne in the middle, tricked in gold.

The walls roughcast, two huge cupboards
lord their cloudstreaked wood;
behind, a plaster Christ dies under a tilt,

his head holed, eyes open on drunks.
And the stink of dripping and grease
rise to his bare heart like bad incense.

# W is for Wolska

Maryla Wolska was born in Lviv in 1873. She studied music and painting, but took to poetry when her eyesight failed. She worked as a field hospital nurse in the First World War, and continued her parents' open house invitation to Polish writers and artists. She died in Lviv in 1930.

## Ex Voto

I know that you will always be
a mist, a dream, no more, to me,
and yet, in moonlight's golden calm
I reach my ever-longing arms
before your shade…

I know that I will always be
a mist, a dream, no more, to me,
and yet in moonlight's golden sleep
I hang my given heart to keep
before your shade…

## My Soul

My soul will last forever as a girl,
a girl who went to the morning forest with a berry-jug,
strong and sure of her beauty, that even when the years have passed
she will be in the fairness of her face forever young…
my soul will last forever as a girl.

My soul in a green-plait garland
walks on the lonely path, free as a forest bird,
awed only at the morning sun,
free as a life-skimming wind,
my soul in a green-plait garland…

My soul I keep from the hands of others;
belonging to itself, nobody else, not known,
I take this girlish heart to some god's Elsewhere,
just as you take a jug of raspberries at evening home –
my soul I keep from the hands of others.

## Prelude

Night… Spring rain… in sleepy gardens
light air steams from damp lilacs… and where the heart is held
hid pulses beat, glowing –
the brief Spring bloom… passes… Summer will come,
waiting night is lapped in weight and blur,
wet, boundless sapphire-stars glitters,
and all about is still, like the eve of some holiday;
and I feel – that my life's most lifted note
has not been sounded yet.

# and for Wolker

Jiří Wolker was born in Prostijov in 1900. In 1923 he was diagnosed with TB, and wrote his own epitaph, promising to transform 'my subjective torments into poetry'. Variously liked and disliked as a Social Realist and/or Bad Ideologue, he succumbed to his lung disease in 1924.

## Things

Things are great. The Quiet Company.
People do with them
like they aren't alive.
But they are. They stare at us
like constant dogs, studying,
hurting.
No one talks to them.
Too shy to talk first,
quiet, waiting, quiet,
still —
they long to talk.

That's why we love Things.
And Every Thing in the world.

## Saint Nicholas Day

It's Saint Nicholas Day.
I'm going home on the Fast Train,
cutting the land-like-mashed-potato look,
sugar and cinnamon sprinkled,
news forgotten, tramlines and streets
in a grey compartment
and people coming and going
heart-bidden.

This Saint's Evening
has made our train a stocking at the window.
Saint Nicholas, come here too,
come to these restless children on their pilgrimage.
They want to travel-hug the land
and with their purposes the sky.
Give them faith-full and consoling words,
please, put rosy apples and golden nuts
into this Prague-Bohumín train,
and all the trains about the world.


**In Love**

A poor man came to you,
it was me.
Woman, what of your wealth will you give me
locked in red lips and white breasts.

Street mud,
heart-hunger,
we must love someone,
man is lonely;
lost amongst many.
I stand, I stand,
can't outstand the words
I would, woman, lay in your hand
simply, reverent,
as a mother lays dinnerplates
on the table.
Poor and rich folks don't get on.

She was beautiful,
looking but could not see.
Terrible golden eyes,
two golden shop windows
yelling
at the needy thieving street.

## Humble

I will get small and then smaller,
till I'm the smallestthingintheworld.

In the summer morning field
I will go to the smallest flower
and whisper while I hug it:
'Little barefoot laddie,
Heaven has leaned on you
with a dewdrop
so it doesn't fall.'


## Postbox

Streetcorner postbox,
not just Anything.
Blue blossom,
much made of,
told such secrets,
letters chucked in this side and that,
sad ones this, cheery that.

White pollen letters
wait for trains and boats, for a man
who will bumblebee and breeze them away
where hearts are,
red stigmas
hiding in rosy petals.
When a letter gets there,
they will fruit,
sour or sweet.

## Back

Bridge lamps
yell glass teeth,
brave old-timers
brag in wine and bar
how many girls bought,
how many men killed –
tonight –
a black river runs
away drowned flowers,
an only-man-in-the-world,
fog, frost, gales
don't say today
where the street is,
that goes to heaven
or home.

Darling, you
switched the far light
white window in a black block.
I am thinking of you,
you asleep with the light on.
And over the bed, like a safe dream,
a hanging curtain.
You don't dream of me
night-walking,
you dream of me
seen, next morning.
How beautiful to prick a little hole in the sky!

But today
I am fated unhappy.
I think of those
who saw in hazy wanderings the saint,
and I must remember those
who never saw him
because they paid for dinner with their eyes.

# X is for Xirinacs

Olga Xirinacs Díaz was born in Tarragona in 1936. She teaches the piano,
and writes, in Catalan, poetry, prose, children's tales, and newspaper
articles.


### Our Daily Fair

Horses, horses while we walk
the city streets!
Bluetail horses,
fretting cotton,
stun-flung manes!
Horses, horses in The Street,
horses wheeling
all the circle of the day.
And if we reach The Balcony
we say our brief goodbye,
and with twilight friends
recatch the beat, the beat
at the door of this, our dream.


### I'm Making a Plate of Olives...

I'm making a plate of olives,
bread and cheese,
russet wine,
that will feed
all the evening talk:
listen to the firewood hour,
unbar the bolt
and reaffirm the old ties
of earth.

## Three Small Songs from the Upper Side

Small Pitxa fountain,
clear shadow,
splash housefronts,
and with smooth hands
bless the time
         of the pomegranate
         of the orange
         of the soutane.


Small stair-vases
under lemons, under figtrees;
eyes and water sicken
when fever breeds
in such wet lands.


Some braids vanish
into soft shadow:
stone toasts almonds
and hazel eyes:
olive skin,
gypsy hands,
dress-billow.


## Students

Days wear away
under a lineal world,
schoolish, mathsy,
sand-edgeless
through strange mirages.

For us the hours pass
and we will leave the skin
beneath the aseptic glass
nailed with dim needles.

## They Grow Blue in Your Skin...

They grow blue in your skin,
not just ultramarine:
the tightened flesh
buzzes with new vibrations,
and guitars
seek the nests
of crickets and lizards.
When your night unleashes, lay the table,
and make a drinking-toast of tar
to dip the angel-bread.

## and for Xenophanes

Xenophanes (of Colophon) was born about 570 BC. He believed his 'philosophy-as-poetry' would live 'in fame through all of Greece, and for as long as Greek poetry lives'. Perhaps sold once into slavery, perhaps burying his sons with his own hands, he may have died, at a ripe age, about 480 BC.


**Bits and Pieces**

One God *Is*, above *all* gods and people,
looking and thinking *nothing like us*

All of God *sees*, All of God *minds*, All of God *hears*

*Minding* and *thinking,* everything goes smoothly by *Him*

and the *Is* always stays in its place, still unmoved,
which is *Right*, not moving from place to place

but people think gods are *Born* like them,
*dress* like, *body* and *talk* like

if *Cows* or *Lions* had hands, and painted pictures
and did *Art* like people *do Art*,
then they would draw *god bodies*
in their own kind like
*horsegods* for horses and *cowgods* for cows

*Homer* and *Hesiod* made gods *Do Things,*
men get tut-tutted and badnamed for
stories with many *Wrong Things* in them,
like *thieving* and *wife-thieving* and *god-deceiving*

and everything comes from *Earth* and ends up there

we all come out of *Earth* and *Water*

everything that is *Born* and *Grows* is *Earth* and *Water*

*Water* and *Wind* come whoosh out of the Sea,
*wind-waves* would never come out of the *Clouds*
and swash around if it were not for the Sea,
river-rush and rainplop would not come out of the Sky
if it were not for the Sea truly the Great Sea is the *Maker*
of *clouds* and *wind* and *river*

and we can see this earth-top-end, our feet on the ground,
but *down there* it slides whoosh away to *Infinity*

there has never been anyone and never will be who
*Knows Exactly* what I think about Gods or anything else,
even if he gets it *sort of Right* by *Guessing* he still
*doesn't know,* but oh everybody *thinks* they know

I think these things look rather like *the Truth*

to start with Gods did not tell people *everything* about *everything*
but we have found out more and more bit by bit by *looking*

here are some *Good Subjects* for a chat when you are
lying on a nice *Sofa* by the fire in winter and having some
*sweet wine* and *lentil pattie* after dinner: *Who Are You and
What's Your Family and How Much Land Have You Got and
How Old Were You When the Medes Came Marching In*

another thing I thought of ah *Once Upon a Time*
there was a Dog that got beaten and a Man passing by
felt sorry for it and he said *Stop beating that dog
because it is the soul of my best friend
I recognised it as soon as I heard its voice*

if you win a *Running Race* or the *5-Eventer* at Olympia
where the *Zeus-grove* waffles by *Pisa's Creek*
or *Wrestling* or *Hurt-Me Boxing* or
*Really-Hurt-Me Ultimate Fighting* people will say
*What a Great Person* and you will get a front seat at
Conference Things and the City will pay for all your fun

at the *Eating* Conference Things and
you will get some *To Die For* present and
if you won something *With a Horse*
then you would still get all these things but
you would not deserve them *Like I Do* because
*Wisdom* is better than *Big Men* and *Big Men-With-Horses*
and I think this way round is *Wrong*
to think strength is better than *Wonderful Wisdom*
and just because there is someone in some city
that is Really Good at *Boxing* or the *5-Eventer* or *Wrestling*
or *Running* which at least is better than things in the Games
that are just *all about Strength* then that city would not be
*Any Better Governed* because of them, so any city should not be
*All that Over the Moon* if one of its men wins at the Games
on the beautiful banks of the *Pisas*
because that would not *Fill the City Coffers*

and they copied the Lydians' *Love of Pathetic Luxuries*
not having a clue what it is like to live under a horrible Tyrant
yet and they paraded into the Market
and *One Thousand* of them *mincing round* in *purple clothes*
showing off wagging their lovely hair
*oiled up* with beautiful smelly creams

now the floor is clean and everyone's hands and all the cups
and one person puts on *all the weavy headwreaths*
and another one passes round the *sweetsmelling cream* in a jar
and the mixbowl is full of *nice wine* and there's more of it
all *smooth* and *light and sweet nearby* in big jugs so it won't
run out and in the middle *frankincense* willows up its *holy smell* and
there is cold sweet pure water and nearby is the *yellowcrust bread*
and the Big Table is full of *Cheese* and *Gorgeous Honey*
and the altar in the middle is all thick with *flowers*
everywhere and everyone is *singing* and *laughing* all
round the house. Now, People Having Fun should
*(a) sing a God-song FIRST, holy words and useful verses*
*(b) pour out properly some offering or other*
*(c) pray for the Strength to Do Good*
*(which is easy enough to do at Home) and THEN*
*(d) they can have a good but not too much Drink*

*with a happy mind* as long as they are not too old
and don't have to get *Carried Home* by a Slave
afterwards and in fact a man who *has a drink* and then *talks
about good things* (usually his *His Memories and Good Works)*
is a Good Man but there is nothing Good about
worbely-borbelling on about *Titan Battles Giant Fights
Centaur Scrums* and all that old *Make-Believe Stuff*
or *plotting nasty revolutions* and you should always give
the Gods Good Respect because that is *Good*

you sent a *Goat's Thigh-Bone* and got a *Big Fat Bull-Leg*
back which is an Excellent Present and All of Greece
will get a bit of Credit for that really and as long as there are
*Poets* to *Poem* they will keep your famousness alive

and no one who is not an *Idiot* would pour *wine into a cup first*
to mix it because *water goes in first* and then *wine on top*

*sixty-seven years* my thinking and ideas and etcetera have been
bandied and batted up and down and round and round Greece
but THAT happened when I was *twenty-five*
if I have got my *Facts Right*

and a *promise like that* is easier to get from a Believer than a *Half-
Believer*

*miles* weaker than a *Really Old Man*

*Bacchussy spine-sticks* are stuck all round the strong walled house

*right from the start* in *Homer's* version because everyone knows them
*off by heart*

and if God had not created *White Honey*
I would have said *Figs* were *miles sweeter*

holy water drabbles down your cave walls

*as many things as THEY have created for Men to Look At*

184

# Y is for Yourcenar

Marguerite Yourcenar was born in Brussels in 1903. She published novels and poems from the age of 18. In 1939 she left to live and work in the USA until 1979. Best-known for her novel *Memoirs of Hadrian*, she was elected to the Académie française in 1980. She died in 1987.

## Written on the Back of Two Postcards

A siren weeps
a ship sails out
on the water where death is.

I suffer this absence
and the hard span;
sadness is a wall.

The way is a catch:
no trains, no ships.
Intentions founder.

Thought, sure arrow,
thrills the distance;
sweetly strikes:
(honey of wounds
embalms the heart).

## Erotic

You the hornet and I the rose,
you the swash and I the rock;
in the odd metamorphosis,
you the Phoenix, I the pyre.

You Narcissus, and I the Spring;
my eyes reflect your disquiet;
you the money and I the purse;
I the wave and the swimmer-self.

And you, lip on the lip,
you the fever-cradle still unstirred,
wave run into waves.

But whatever game this softly is,
the soul takes flight in fire each time,
bright golden bird, into the far blue sky.


## Fitful

The failing sun blurs amongst the mist;
my love has gone down like a mortal star.
Along the shabby quays blind night relumes;
my heart is old as Herod and his sin.

Each that lives, hub of a hidden world,
victim and hangman, beats his pain upon an anvil;
and the grey faces are splats of spray
in the black and human wave upon the swelling asphalt.

Love, where are we? Are we sure of being?
And the moon that turns pale for its pity of man
sobs in silver on the empty edges of the roofs.

And the maddened eye of town watches, unwanting,
luminous–cold and fixedly achange,
this star already dead and whiter than life.

## Poem for a Doll Bought in a Russian Market

Me
I am
royal blue
and sooty black

I am the Mighty Moor
(foe of Petrushka).
Night is my troika;
the sun is my golden ball.

Nearly as huge as the shadows,
but all breakable as a living thing,
the littlest breath riots my spineless frame.

I am quite indifferent, for I am rather wise:
do not mock my swart, my blooming lips,
I am, as you, a puppet held in giant hands.


## Hermaphrodite

Done as one and double-venery,
delicious-impassive, the nub of everything;
sexes, mind and flesh, quick effects and longer causes,
the shifting plural fixes at the singular.

In this dismemberment that is the fact,
the parted beings join in this once more;
the sweet and perfect monster couched in roses;
desire the sculptor, pleasure what is made.

Happiness togethered in the smooth, hard flesh;
the fair, reclining marble just a longer kiss;
seven notes as one have made two chords.

And closing now its eyes, half-shade and fire,
amongst the tender carelessness of god who would be woman,
he offers to desire the puzzle of his body.

## and for Yavorov

Peyo (P.K.) Yavorov was born in Chirpan in 1878. Called 'the King of Despair', he worked tirelessly for the liberation of Bulgaria and Macedonia from the Ottoman Empire. His two loves died young, and Yavorov followed the second in a self-poisoning and pistol suicide in Sofia in 1914.

### Clouds

Dark clouds: ah,
leave the sky not gloomed!
Dark thoughts: oh,
leave the heart not galled!

Clouds: and a squalled gale's blow
with them.
Thoughts: and a stale song
dopes them.

### Confession

From the sun's first morning
I began to learn (learn?):
how to love, and sing,
and wholly live.

To the last dark's evening
I did not learn (not learn):
loved many, sang much,
and little lived.

## Pardon

That look goodbye, brimmed with blame
and sadness, overloads me;
and I fail, fall and long
on one remembered thing.

We held our kinder hearts away,
we held away our words;
our hearts knew one another,
our hearts knew us always.

We could have been happy.
That could have been – not a dream.
God alone looked after us.
And now – all black-alone.

That last look, too swiftly soon;
a cloud dimmed at me.
I clutched at, sorely cried,
yelled… too late, too late.

Blame me. Anger
and ill. Remember –
O well-revenged and unfallen –
and pardon.


## Two Souls

I do not live, but burn. Two
loathing souls box in my heart:
angel and devil. And their
firesnort parches me there.

Whatever I light on bursts two-flamed,
in every stone I hear two hearts;
and everywhere two loggerheads,
pained-apart, that whisper away in ash.

And behind me the wind shifts the ashes
over my unsettled never–wasness.
I do not only live, but burn: to leave
an ashdrift down the dark forever.

# Z is for Zhadovskaya

Yulia Zhadovskaya was born in Yaroslavl Province in 1824, with one missing arm and the other's fingers fused. She lived and studied with her aunt, the poet Anna Gotovtsova, whose daughter became her amanuensis. Her portrait was painted by Nikolay Lavrov. She married at 38, and never wrote again. She died in 1883.

## In Difference

My love, you will forget me now,
though I remember you;
whilst you exchange new loves for old,
my sunny day of love is done.

Different faces smile at you,
new friends will come and go,
and thoughts renew, and you will find
new happiness instead of mine.

Whilst I, in quiet sadness, take
the hapless, darker way,
and how I love, and how I weep
the grave alone at last shall know.

## On a Track

Sadly I stare at the road,
my path is narrow and hard!
I fail in my hope and my heart,
and I long for my long-due rest.

Distance bids fair no more,
few are well-met on the way,
too often I journey matched
with the foolish, the proud and the brute.

And often I have been caught
by the bitter, the cheap and the false,
who poisoned my footsore soul,
and crushed the bright colours of life.

Though some companions were good,
they faded slowly behind...
and I, abandoned and tired,
traipse the hard track alone!


## Evening

Silence is everywhere; and nature sleeps
and in the sky the far stars gently burn!
The sun fades slowly in the distant west,
the clouds go, slow and patient, on their way.
O that my sickened soul might find some joy
in such a soft, companionable light
as now the evening star lets brightly fall!
Ah, why am I so dark, and full of pain?
Who can sweeten now my bitter heart?
I hope for nothing, think of nothing past;
what is in my soul?... the whole world sleeps;
no answer comes... only the glittered line
of some fire-falling star before my eyes.


## The Sway of Sounds

That song they sang a day ago
will still not leave my mind;
it fills me still with gloomy thoughts,
I still hear suffering and pain.
Today I wished to work again,

but hardly was my needle touched
when darkness moved upon my eyes
and bowed my head upon my breast;
and like some foul disease, those sounds
took heavy hold upon my soul,
and bore my heart in pain away.
And still I whispered, 'Love, I love…'

## and for Zetlitz

Jens Zetlitz was born in Stavanger in 1761. His poems generally celebrate the pleasant effects of alcohol and patriotism. He studied theology in Copenhagen (spending much time at the Norwegian Society there, speaking, drinking, poeticising and singing patriotic songs) and returned to Norway as an ordained minister. He died in his ministry in Kviteseid in 1821. There is a street named after him in Stavanger.

### Grapes were Made to Grin the World...

Grapes were made to grin the world,
  Fillerup!
Cultivated, squashed and swull,
  Fillerup!
And Good God Evan's tank-ah-ard
is Heaven mixed with Earthly Gifts!
  Gedditdown! Fillerupagain!
  Glass gone! Fillerupagain!
  Gedditdown!

He tiptooth forth and Pain desists,
  Fillerup!
He sprinkles roses 'mongst life's thorns,
  Fillerup!
He smootheth Envy's pasty faith
and tameth Lion and Lofty Lassie,
  Gedditdown! Fillerupagain!
  Glass gone! Fillerupagain!
  Gedditdown!

When oomph is sleeping, get your glass!
  Fillerup!
And when the World's ole suit don't fit!
  Fillerup!

Thus oomph arises, Go gets up
and You and This old World shake hands,
   Gedditdown! Fillerupagain!
   Glass gone! Fillerupagain!
   Gedditdown!

Has some Endow'wed Doris gotcha?
   Fillerup!
Have a liddle drink – gerrup –
   Fillerup!
And tell her straight how 'ard ye burn,
and watch her Art fall 'elpless *flop*
   Gedditdown! Fillerupagain!
   Glass gone! Fillerupagain!
   Gedditdown!


**It Went Like This**

Pain (son of Anger)
hiked gruesome in,
and sowed his spunk
in every heart.

Moans and praying
moaned and prayed
from us Earth men
to our Earth God.

The Big Creator heard
his wee Creation's cry
and, touched with tears,
he drew up some advice.

He made us
Love and Happiness,
and for weeping
he gave us grapes.

And with them Hope
all sprouted out,
and Love's lighthats
were lit lit lit.

Fools still moan,
ah Life! oh me!:
me, I shall pursue anew
Love made, and Happiness.

## My Longings

How little it takes
to be happy:
bright thoughts, girl's smile,
friend's regard,
little house to lie low in,
good bread, clean water,
and all the use of them
with understanding.

Gold has gleam, the sword might,
and rank some honour;
it's nice to be clever,
but it is not the thing.
No, no; fear no fool's sentence,
take the day as it comes;
it is more than gold or honour.

Oh, in Elisa's arms
I can say to the world,
'I have wrapped up in me, O Earth,
your best girl';
and a friend by my side,
happy in my happiness –
then I want nothing more,
though outcast and poor.

I found far a lonesome valley,
I built a little house;
my girl, my friend and me,
shut in, shut off.
I made the land fruitful,
and hymned His goodness,
the High-Sat in Heaven, in sweat,
and made my circle full –

a father! – dear children
on my work-ached knees,
and with grasping,
searching eyes
found a mother's looks,
and kissed away child-tears.
I knew the world. I saw great God,
who set me here.

I said to the little and brave,
'Virtue is the greatest joy;
sin the greatest shame.'
I said to the little two,
'Roses grow in thorns,
happiness pours from Virtue's spring,
and God will make you happy.'

# Acknowledgements

I would like to thank the following people for their patient and self-less help in the finding and first translating of the poems in this book.

Akhmatova/Apukhtin/Kapnist/Parnok/Tyutchev/Zhadovskaya –
  Tamara Romanyk
Boye/Fröding – Charlotte Linder
Baudelaire/Marie de France/Hamoir/Laforgue/Maeterlinck/
  Noailles/Nerval/Queen Mary/Renaud/Tiburge/Vivien/
  Verhaeren/Yourcenar – Kurt Ganzl
Corinna – a nineteenth-century translation by P. Rowson
Carducci/Pasolini/Quasimodo – Favorita '69
Dehmel – Emmanuel George
Droste-Húlshoff/Lasker-Schüler – Debbie James
Espanca – John Havelda
Eluard – Jacinta and Tony Barnard
Guglielminetti – Anne Swan, Patricia Hardin, Alessandro
  Anghinoni
Giusti – Aimee Paul
Hofmannsthal – Minna Simpson
Isanos/Ioanid – Cris Constantinescu
Jorunn – John Lucas
Jacobsen – Alice Bendtner
Konopnika/Wolska – Basia Jaworski
Lasker-Schüler/Otto-Peters – Oliver Lesky
Maksimovic – Michael Vincent
Olafssons – Jen Fredericks
Radauskas – C.L. Strom
Salinas – Lisa Martin, Leslie Portas
Södergran – Thom Milius, Anne Milius
Ullmann – Thomas Zaufke
Uhland – Peter Salmons
Wolker – Irene Jasikova
Xenophanes – a 1923 translation by the Rev. A.M. Morton
Xirinacs – Anna Vives
Yavorov – Maria Ovtcharova

Zetlitz – Stian Gustavsen

For helping to find people finding people: David Bircumshaw, Nancy Gallas, Greg Beaven, Val Moore, Kerry Featherstone, Anna Besley, Mark Goodwin, Patti Oliver, and Nikki Clayton.

The poems were turned first into plain, literal, line-by-line English versions by the people acknowledged above, then re-poemed by me. None of the poems was chosen by me. Each one was sent to or chosen by a translator from what they or I had found.

Further information on all the poets in this book is available on the internet.

# Index of Titles

# Index of First Lines